Language and popular culture in Japan

日本 研究 Japanese Studies

Brian Moeran

Language
and popular culture
in Japan

Manchester University Press
Manchester and New York
Distributed exclusively in the USA and Canada by St Martin's Press

Copyright © Brian Moeran 1989

Published by Manchester University Press
Oxford Road, Manchester M13 9PL, UK
and Room 400, 175 Fifth Avenue,
New York, NY 10010, USA

*Distributed exclusively in the USA and Canada
by* St. Martin's Press, Inc.,
175 Fifth Avenue, New York, NY10010, USA

British Library cataloguing in publication data
Moeran, Brian
    Language and popular Culture in Japan.—(Japanese
Studies).
    1. Japanese popular culture
    I. Title   II. Series
    306'.1

Library of Congress cataloging in publication data
Moeran, Brian.
    Language and popular culture in Japan/Brian Moeran.
        p.   cm.—(Japanese studies)
    Includes index.
    ISBN 0-7190-3041-2
    1. Japan—Popular culture.   2. Language and culture—Japan.
I. Title.   II. Series.
DS821.M6398   1989
306'.4'0952—dc19   89-2793

ISBN 0 7190 3041 2 *hardback*

*Printed in Great Britain
    by Billings of Worcester*

Contents

For DAVID

Preface

> A number of things, I think are true. One is that there has been an enormous amount of genre mixing in intellectual life in recent years, and it is, such blurring of kinds, continuing apace. Another is that many social scientists have turned away from a laws and instances idea of explanation towards a cases and interpretations one, looking less for the sort of thing that connects planets and pendulums and more for the sort that connects chrysanthemums and swords.

So wrote Clifford Geertz at the beginning of his pursuit for 'local knowledge' (1983: 19). Given the recent criticisms of Ruth Benedict's famous study of Japan, Geertz's choice of metaphor is perhaps unfortunate, but one can only sympathise with his approach. As a social anthropologist I, too, have participated in this blurring of genres by focusing on the relation between language and popular culture in contemporary Japanese society. Neither 'sociological' enough for most anthropologists, nor rigorous enough for those better versed than I in linguistics, and only semi-otic at best in its analyses of various aspects of poular culture, I suspect that this book—like others that I have written—will fall between at least three of the *zabuton* cushions occupied by my academic colleagues. For this I can only beg their indulgence (in the typical Japanese manner of *amae*) and pray that some unknown reader 'out there' will find this book of more than passing interest.

Of course, so much has been written about Japan recently that potential readers are forgiven for heaving a sigh as they put this volume back on the bookstore shelf, and turn their thoughts to 'higher' literature. Over the past decades, Japan has been so exoticised and orientalised—both by Westerners and by the Japanese themselves—that it is hard to tell whether those whom we call the 'Japanese' are 'real' people, or a nation acting out a part written for them by Western civilisation. That, I think, is the underlying problem tackled in this book, although, being short of both ideas and scholarship, I am afraid that I have failed to solve it entirely to my satisfaction.

Let me be clear about two things right from the start. Firstly, I do not in this book attempt to discuss the 'artistic' status of popular culture in Japanese society. In other words, I am not concerned with whether, by some machination of language, folk crafts or films form a new art, to be placed in the realm of 'high' culture. Secondly, I have in general talked of popular culture in the singular, as a kind of monolithic entity, rather than of the more pluralistic popular *cultures*. In this respect, I may be accused of having surrendered my intellectual faculties to that very ideology of cultural 'homogeneity' that I attack in this book. However, it so happened that all of those popular cultural forms with which I here deal fitted into a single monolithic category. Moreover, the examples of such social groups as those of the *yakuza* gangsters and *burakumin* 'outcasts' suggest that there is a strong tendency for marginal groups to embrace mainstream ideals and thereby become more central to the workings of Japanese society. I think that the same goes for popular cultural forms, whose cultures are rapidly assimilated into a single culture.

What I have tried to do, then, is take one 'myth'—that of the Japanese language—and use it to demystify other ideologies, such as the notion that the group is more important than the individual, in contemporary Japanese society. I have chosen to emphasise popular culture, because it is one of the few things about Japan that that non-existent entity, the 'person' in the street, actually 'knows' something about. Who has not followed *sumō* on TV, practised at some stage or other one of the martial arts, or been to see a *samurai* film? Japan is widely known these days for its architecture, fashion, *pachinko* slot machines, and *geisha*—the last of which has, like 'geyser', the dubious distinction of being pronounced in at least three ways—two of them fiendish! For all this interest (which has, alas, often been as misguided as people's bastardisation of the Japanese phonetic system), there have until recently been very few books devoted to aspects of Japan's popular culture. Buruma (1984), of course, is the major exception, but his theme is primarily that of sexuality and sex—a theme in which I myself, as someone who is in the process of going through his 'manopause', have a great interest (see Chapters 8 and 11), but which, as an academic who now occupies a hitherto respected University Chair (with swivel seat and at least five wheels), I feel duty bound to suggest has certain theoretical limitations. Even in Japan, life is not *all* wine, women and song—as the potters of Sarayama will ably testify.

So perhaps, after all, my 'semi-linguapological' approach does have some merit. Each of the chapters deals with one way in which language is used in various kinds of popular culture—from *sake* drinking, where conversation gives way to inebriated song and the occasional punch-up, to *jidaigeki* in which the efficacy of language is actually denied. *En route*, I have occasionally attempted to see where that undisciplined discipline of anthropology itself fits into the themes revealed by Japan's popular culture, and have laid the occasional wired barb to trip up those who might feel tempted by loyalty to the cause of planets and pendulums to indulge in a minor form of trench warfare. One needs a sense of humour to survive the ordeal of writing a book, especially when the word processor decides to devour, without warning, whole chunks of carefully prepared and peppered prose. And not even a belch to show for it!

Brian Moeran

Speak Japan, Japanspeak

Introduction

'*Fuck me quick! The barbarians are coming.*' It is not often that one gets an invitation of this kind—especially from a middle-aged woman wearing this message on her T shirt in a commuter train near Osaka. In an idle moment, perhaps, one might be excused for wondering whether the 'barbarians' referred to would have been translated into Japanese as '*yabanjin*' or the more opprobrious '*ketō*' ('red-haired devils'). One might also question whether the wearer of this splendid T shirt really was as old as she looked, or whether a number of those sallow-faced men in soiled suits, who spend their time poring over erotic magazines in commuter trains, had not perhaps taken undue advantage of the lady's request.

Be that as it may, this is probably a more extreme example of the kind of usage to which English can be put in Japan—especially on such articles as T shirts and shopping bags. But the reader should also realize that there are quite a few young people in Europe and the United States whose Chinese-character printed T shirts emit equally ridiculous messages. *Yūmei* (有名) is a popular phrase for the anonymous youth hopefully grasping for 'fame', while *nyō* (尿), meaning 'urine', could well be interpreted as a sign to the world to 'piss off'. Once again, it would seem as if the dulcet tones of Japanese harmony (albeit in brief physical exercise in a love hotel) have been matched by Western discord!

It is on the way in which language is used in popular cultural forms, then, that this book concentrates. The focus, too, is on *Japanese* popular culture, although I do make comparisons with Britain when it comes to advertising slogans, and also look at Japanese as it has been adopted abroad (in the form of Californian car licence plates). In fact, the *Fuck me quick* ... message quoted above is somewhat exceptional; it has a directness for which Japanese in general is not renowned. Take a glance, for example, at those beautifully colour-printed tear-off stickers that adorn telephone booths in Japan's entertainment areas. *Cinderella, Second Love, Madonna, Sweet Pea, Poem, Melon, Essence, Secret, Scanty,* and *Rabbit* (a *Playboy* in disguise?) are some examples collected before the stickers were removed and the booths cleaned by an employee of Japan's telephone corporation early the next morning. How fresh, naive and innocent they seem, compared with those hastily hand-scrawled messages that deface British Telecom equipment near London's hotel ghettoes: *Stiletto Mistress, New Rubber Lover, Mistress Cane,* and *Man Trainer.* There are, of course, one or two more gentle names—*Ebony Eyes,* for example, or *Paradise, Easter Chick, Brown Sugar* and *Magnifico* —but in England the customer knows what he is getting, whether it be a *Mutual caning, Stimulating black massage, Breast relief with busty blonde,* or *Kinky uniform fun.* No opportunity here for *Change OK,* available to the dissatisfied customer in Japan.

It is in this kind of indirectness, and the symbolism that attaches to the vagueness of words in Japanese, that I am here primarily interested. The examples—*sake* drinking, advertising slogans and tourist brochures, to name but three—may be disparate, but the argument is simple. Language, as used in popular culture and elsewhere, is a form of dominant ideology designed to sustain a myth that emphasises 'Japaneseness'. In this respect, it maintains the cultural gulf between 'East' and 'West', and encourages the Japanese to indulge in a form of inverse 'orientalism' (Said 1977).[1]

Hitherto, almost all of the writing concerning the use of language in Japanese society has been 'syntagmatic' in style. In other words, it has adopted a 'microlevel' approach which views the use of language in everyday social relations, and attempts to gauge in what way language does, or does not, parallel social behaviour. I intend to run through this literature in the remaining part of this chapter: firstly, because there may be some readers unfamiliar with it; and secondly, because the arguments put forward about how group boundaries are marked out by linguistic usage are important to an understanding of a second, 'macrolevel' approach that I here espouse. What interests me is the way in which social ideals are reflected in the *keywords* used to describe such different

2

phenomena as sports, aesthetics, and film. In this manner, I hope to combine the essentially 'syntagmatic' approach of sociolinguistics with the more 'paradigmatic' approach of recent anthropology (*cf*. Ardener 1971: lxxvi-lxxvii).

Pronominal usage

Discussions of Japanese society by anthropologists and other social scientists tend to focus on such oppositions as 'frame' and 'attribute' (Nakane 1970: 1), 'ideology' (*tatemae*) and 'actuality' (*honne*), 'front' (*omote*) and 'back' (*ura*) (Johnson 1980), 'in' (*uchi*) and 'out' (*soto*) (Ishida 1984), and of course, group and individual. As a whole, these oppositions may be subsumed under the title of *nihonjinron*. Recently, however, the arguments put forward by such famous scholars as Benedict, Nakane and Doi have been roundly criticised for presenting Japanese society in ideal, rather than actual, terms. In particular, the ideals of harmony, hierarchy, homogeneity and group loyalty have been subject to hard scrutiny. Is Japanese society as devoid of conflict as some would make out? Are the Japanese really as homogeneous as they seem? Can they act only within the vertical framework of a small group?

One of the more frequently advocated points in this so-called 'group model' of Japanese society (Befu 1980) is that social organisation is based upon vertical, rather than horizontal, relations. The aim of the rest of this chapter is to show that language use does *not* simply reflect vertical relations between people but points to the existence of in- and out-groups of a more horizontal nature. It is as a means of explaining the social process of solidarity and differentiation, therefore, that the microlevel approach is here adopted. At the same time, we can see how language *use* in fact both supports and threatens the dominant linguistic *ideology* of 'Japaneseness'.

The use of pronouns in social interaction has been seen by a number of sociolinguists to be vital to any discussion of hierarchy—particularly class—in Western societies. A shift in the usage of singular and plural second person pronouns—of, for example, *tu* and *vous* in France or French-speaking Canada—can signify

3

long-term changes in social relations. The fact that customers at French restaurants no longer use the depreciatory *tu* when addressing a waiter reflects a growing classlessness in French society; the use of reciprocal *tu* or *vous* between parent and child shows the changing nature of upper-class families in contemporary French society (*cf.* Brown and Gilman 1960; Lambert 1972).

One of the features of Japanese is a marked *absence* of pronominal usage. Instead of saying 'I will go to a *pachinko* parlour', or 'he read a *manga* comic', a Japanese will often simply say '(will) go' (*ikimasu*), or 'read it' (*yomimashita*), and leave it to the person to whom s/he is speaking to work out from the context precisely who is doing what. It is, of course, the grammatical structure of the Japanese language which enables a speaker to do this, since the subject of the sentence can be subsumed in the verb form, but we should note that it is quite possible for someone to introduce a personal pronoun should s/he so desire. In other words, '*I will go*' (*watashi* or *boku ga/wa ikimasu*) is acceptable, and may even be necessary when the speaker wishes to emphasise either the agent or the action in the phrase spoken. In this respect, words for 'I' (*wata[ku]shi*) or 'you' (*anata*) are not strictly speaking 'pronouns', since they do not 'stand in stead of' nouns. Rather, they follow the rules applicable to nouns in Japanese grammar (*cf.* Miller 1967: 335). For this reason, perhaps, we should call pronouns 'personal referents' in that they are:

> 'nouns that indicate categories and degrees of communicative distance. The selection of one from among the great array of such referents will reflect the human and social relationships that pertain between the two parties. There are no fixed points, either 'self' or 'other', and ... it is of the utmost significance that designation of the other invariably precedes designation of the self in any interaction' (Smith 1983: 77).

In general, personal referents are avoided wherever possible because, by so doing, a speaker takes the emphasis off certain individuals and their actions, and so breaks down the divisive opposition that tends to exist in communication between 'self' and 'other'. As one might expect from my earlier mention of the relationship between group and individual, the Japanese wish, wherever possible, to create a sense of community. By avoiding the use of personal referents, they are able to establish a 'selflessness' which contributes greatly towards in-group identity.

Another means of creating an in-group solidarity, without having to resort to personal referents which might create a sense of differentiation among people within the group concerned, is by use of *role terms*. To some extent, of course, to refer to one's section head at work as *kachō* is to accept, and possibly to emphasise, the latter's superior position and the hierarchical relations that exist in a company's organisation. But, at the same time, use of a role term serves to stress that relationships between speakers are framed in the group context of the company, or section. This can hardly be said of employees in an American or European company, where either a title and surname, or perhaps a first name only, will be used. Any of these forms can emphasise hierarchy, but first names may be used by juniors who wish to emphasise what they see as the essentially egalitarian nature of human relations. But, whatever the mode of address adopted, it is always the relation between the two individuals involved in the act of communication which is hinted at—never the group context of the place of employment.

One social institution where there does seem to be a degree of cross-cultural similarity in modes of address is the *family*. In American, English or Japanese families, almost all children call their parents 'father' and 'mother' (or by some equivalent forms), and they will probably use other kin terms such as 'uncle', 'aunt', 'grandad' and 'grandma'. In the Japanese family system, elder brothers and sisters will also be addressed by kin terms, rather than by first names (which are reserved to address younger siblings). This in itself can be said to show the greater overall emphasis on the institution of the family in Japan, and on solidarity between its members, compared with their counterparts in most Western societies.

This solidarity is strengthened by the way in which Japanese use kin terms to *refer to themselves* as well as to address others. Fischer (1964) has described how, in the context of the Japanese family, a man will refer to himself as 'father' (*tōchan*) and to his wife as 'mother' (*kāchan*) when talking to his son. This is something we in the West might do sometimes when using baby talk, but generally not otherwise. In other words, as children grow up, we tend to define each member of a family unit by his or her individual characteristics, rather than by the role that s/he plays in the family. In Japan, on the other hand, there is a tendency for senior members of the family to structure relations from the point of view of the youngest child (preferably a boy). This child-centred viewpoint shows the importance, perhaps, that the Japanese still attribute to family relations—an importance which is borne out by the fact that children are addressed and referred to by name or kinship role, rather than by use of personal referent. The fact that Japanese children are taught to master about half a dozen terms of self-reference by the age of six, and that none of the options available is dominant, reveals how early the flexible nature of 'personhood' or 'self' is encouraged in Japanese society (*cf.* Smith 1983: 79).

It is not that Japanese *never* use personal referents unless they absolutely have to. There are occasions when they do wish to differentiate themselves from their interlocutors, and when they will, therefore, make use of personal referents. However, in this case, they will frequently use *group-oriented*, rather than personal, referents. In other words, instead of saying 'I' or 'you' in the singular form, they will use such phrases as *uchi* or *o-taku*, which literally mean 'my house' and 'your house', to refer to individuals. It would probably be more appropriate to translate them with the plural 'we' and 'you', but the point to realise here is the fact that the Japanese, when using these personal referents, are frequently distinguishing between *groups*, rather than between themselves and their interlocutors as individuals, and that they are referring to themselves as *representatives* of such groups. To say '*uchi*' to someone is to intimate that the speaker belongs to a household, hamlet, company section, or even whole company (*cf.* Cole 1971: 172) to which the other (*o-taku*) does not belong. In this respect, *uchi* and *o-taku* are both individually *and* group oriented (*cf.* Bachnik 1982: 14–15), and there is no fixed point from which an individual can break out and identify his, or her, self (Smith 1983: 81).

Honorific usage

That the Japanese are able to dispense with personal referents when talking to one another is in large part a result of the subtle nuances available to them through honorific, or status, language (Miller 1967: 274).[2] As anyone who has tried to master Japanese will know, one of the more difficult aspects of communication centres on which of a variety of verbs and verb forms one should use when addressing or referring to other people. Here we are concerned not simply with lexical items,[3] as in the case of pronominal usage, but with whole styles of speech which are in part determined by the relative status and familiarity of the conversants. *Keigo*, as honorific language is called in Japanese, thus expresses both vertical (status differences and deference) and horizontal (politeness and intimacy) relations.[4]

The major problem facing anybody conversing in Japanese is a choice of speech levels. In the discussion of pronominal usage above, two examples were cited, making use of the verbs 'go' and 'do'. The translation given of 'I will go' (to a *pachinko* parlour) was *ikimasu*, and of 'he read' (*a manga* comic) *yomimashita*. The use of the -⟨i⟩*masu* verb ending in fact expresses a certain level of politeness, and, at a more informal level, could have been written *iku* or *yonda* respectively. All in all, there are three *styles* of speech—plain (-⟨r⟩*u*), polite (-⟨i⟩*masu*), and deferential (*gozaimasu*)—and the choice of which of these to use depends ultimately on the speaker's attitude towards the person s/he is addressing. Life is further complicated by the fact that a Japanese speaker is also offered the choice of humble (*o-* ... *-i suru*), neutral (-⟨r⟩*u*), and exalted (*o-* ... *-i ni naru*) *expressions*. Which of these will be used depends primarily on the speaker's attitude towards the subject of the expression being used (Martin 1964: 409).

From this it can be seen that honorific language in Japanese differs according to whether it is found in what Martin calls an 'axis of address' or an 'axis of reference' (*cf.* also Miller 1967: 270). In other words, the Japanese use different verb forms when they speak *to* someone and when they speak *about* someone, and the question that arises here is what criteria are used by speakers in order to arrive at the 'correct' level of speech. Martin (*ibid.* p. 411) suggests that there are four factors which come into play, and that their relative importance varies according to whether they are used in address or reference. In address, he reckons that 'out-groupness' is the most important factor determining speech level and that this is followed by 'position', 'age' and 'sex' in that order.[5] In reference, however, 'position' is most likely to influence choice of speech level, being followed by the other factors of 'age', 'sex' and 'out-groupness' respectively.

This argument may be illustrated by an example concerning a

secretary talking *to* her boss. She would use an exalted expression, together with a deferential style, appropriate to her own low status, and to his position as president of the company. If, later on in the day, she were asked by a fellow member of the company about the president's whereabouts, the secretary would probably use an exalted expression *about* her boss, but a polite, or possibly plain, style *to* the person speaking to her. If, however, a visitor were to arrive from elsewhere and inquire after the company president, the secretary would use a *humble* (albeit polite) expression about her boss. Precisely because the visitor is an outsider, the secretary places her boss and herself in the same in-group, using a humble expression to signify the visitor's superior status. This is how the principle of 'out-groupness' influences selection of which honorific form to use in conversational interaction.

It can be seen from this example that there are two axes of choice in deciding which linguistic forms to use in Japanese social interaction: one, the axis of formality, works along a continuum which places people in a psychologically close or distant relationship; the other, the axis of deference, deals with people on a continuum of humility and exaltation. Thus, as Bachnik points out (1982: 21), 'in choosing verbal forms the Japanese speaker is defining *two* aspects of relationship along a continuum: degree of closeness and degree of deference'. Honorific language thus makes it possible for a Japanese speaker 'to be close (or intimate) *and* deferential; as well as distant and deferential. It is possible to be close and not deferential (plain) and distant and not deferential. But it is not possible to speak without defining one's relationship vis-a-vis the addressee'. It is because speech interaction in Japanese makes it virtually impossible for people to use words in a neutral manner that they are obliged to resort to complicated ways of speaking in order not to offend those with whom they are communicating (*cf.* Smith 1983: 75−6).[6]

Uchi/soto and omote/ura

It can be seen from the above that there comes a point in interpersonal relations in Japanese society where the hierarchy found in any large group is subordinated to the more important principle of group solidarity in the face of an out-group. The significance of this is that, despite the frequent scholarly discussion of hierarchical relations, *nobody* is ever *absolutely* in an inferior or a superior position in the hierarchy. In the end, it seems as if differentiation among individuals, based on such factors as age, sex and social position, is always subordinated to the principle of in/out-groupness.

This process of solidarity and differentiation is made more explicit in the distinctions Japanese make between *uchi* ('inside') and *soto* ('outside'), on the one hand, and *omote* ('front' or 'public') and *ura* ('back' or 'private'), on the other (*cf.* Lebra 1976: 112–13). As was mentioned above, people will use the group referent '*uchi*' to talk about themselves *vis-à-vis* others, and the general distinction between in- and out-groups is vital to any discussion of Japanese social organisation. But it should be pointed out here that it is the *flexibility* of the boundary between in-group and out-group which needs to make us wary of any explanatory model which sees Japanese society in terms of one monolithic 'group'. Alternately expanding and contracting, rather like an amoeba, the shifting line between inside and outside helps create competitiveness and opposition between groups,[7] as well as diminish conflict within any one group.

The distinction between *omote* and *ura* is frequently encountered in geographical as well as in social relations. For example, the Japanese divide their country into two main parts: *omote nihon*, the eastern seaboard of Japan along the Pacific coast (which includes Tokyo, Nagoya, Osaka and Kyoto); and *ura nihon*, which covers the less developed stretch of coastline facing the Japan Sea. Although *omote nihon* is the centre of everything that goes on in contemporary Japanese society, the Japanese themselves suggest that *ura nihon* is the repository of a traditional way of life and values that represent the 'true' Japan. In other words, what is '*omote*' is in fact a superficial veneer, while '*ura*' is closer to the 'inner reality' of the Japanese character. This distinction is borne out by a number of linguistic metaphors which suggest that in Japan it is easy to be deceived by appearances (*cf.* Moeran 1985a).[8]

In many respects, then, the distinction between *omote* and *ura* is equivalent to a distinction between 'public' and 'private', 'form' and 'content', and 'authority' and 'power' (Johnson 1980)—a point to which I shall return in the next chapter when I discuss *sake*-drinking parties in a Japanese pottery community. At the same time, it ties in with another pair of words used by the Japanese to describe their behaviour—*tatemae* ('principle') and *honne* ('actuality')—and comes close to the sociological distinction between 'group' and 'social exchange' models of Japanese social organisation. It is in fact the combination of *uchi* and *omote* which gives rise to the kind of harmony and consensus that typifies the group model of Japanese society. As Johnson (1980: 93) puts it: '*omote* is an arena where surprises should not occur'. Once feelings break out into the sphere of *soto*, however, we find that conflict can, and frequently does, exist.

In fact, both *omote* and *ura* can mean any one of three things: publicly legitimate *vis-à-vis* privately allowed; dramatised and dignified *vis-à-vis* practical and efficient; and formal and rigid *vis-à-vis* informal and flexible (Ishida 1984: 21). According to Ishida (*ibid.* p. 17), whether one uses *omote* or *ura* in conversation depends to a large extent on the vertical relations that exist between communicants. *Uchi/soto*, however, express in/out group communication of a more horizontal nature.

Lebra (1976: 112) suggests that a combination of *uchi* and *ura* will occur in intimate, *soto* and *omote* in ritual, and *soto* and *ura* in anomic, situational domains.

> In the intimate situation, Ego both perceives Alter as an insider and feels sure that his behavior toward Alter is protected from public exposure. Opposed to the intimate situation is the ritual situation, where Ego perceives Alter as an outsider and is aware that he is performing his role on a stage with Alter or a third person as audience. Confidentiality, which characterizes the intimate situation, is lacking in the ritual situation. Finally, the anomic situation contrasts with the intimate situation in that Ego defines Alter as an outsider, which rules out intimacy between Ego and Alter; it contrasts with the ritual situation in that Ego is freed from the concern that an audience is watching his behavior. The anomic situation is likely to occur when Ego finds Alter or a third person to be a stranger or enemy who does not share Ego's norms and whose approval is irrelevant to Ego. It is in this sense that the anomic situation combines *soto* and *ura*. (*ibid.* p. 113)

What needs to be emphasised is that the distinctions alluded to here do not form a neat set of binary categories, with well-defined rules of when, or when not, to use a certain form of communication. Rather, they parallel the flexibility of social organisation and, indeed, of the Japanese sense of 'self' as a whole (*cf.* Smith 1983: 68–105). But how does the distinction between in-group and out-group, and the important principle of 'out-groupness', affect everyday language use in contemporary Japanese society? One way in which we can see it working is in kinship terminology. A child will address its mother or father, elder sister or brother with an exalted expression (*o-kāsan* or *o-tōsan, o-nēsan* or *o-nīsan*). When talking to people outside its immediate family circle, however, it will use humble expressions for them (*haha, chichi, ane* or *ani* respectively).

The use of what are called 'donatory' verbs (*ageru, yaru, kureru* and so on) is another clear marker of in-groups and out-groups in Japanese society (*cf.* Loveday 1982: 57–9). One of the niceties of Japanese as a language is that people can very rarely just 'do' (*suru*) things; they almost always find themselves doing things 'for someone' (*shite ageru*). A tea ceremony teacher does not simply 'teach' (*oshieru*) his pupils; he 'gives' them the benefit of his teaching (*oshiete ageru, oshiete yaru*). A housewife does not just 'look at' (*miru*) a yard of homespun cloth in a department store; she asks to be 'given' the opportunity to look at it (*misete moraeru, misete itadakeru*). Almost every action that takes place between individuals, therefore, becomes a matter of mutual reciprocity, and the exact position in which these individuals stand in relation to each other is marked by the humble, neutral or exalted form of an 'out-giving' (*ageru* or *yaru*) or 'in-giving' (*kureru* or *kudasaru*) verb.

It can be seen here that in fact donatory verbs and kinship terms are structurally very similar to personal referents, in that they present the speaker with a dual perspective in defining his or her 'self': one of location, the other of reference (*cf.* Bachnik 1982: 7). In this respect, the relationship between speaker and addressee is not so much one of *contrast* (typical of European languages), as of *mutuality* (*ibid.* p. 10).

11

The Japanese language, then, helps pinpoint precisely one person's social relationship with another. It reveals Japanese society to be full of secret and overt groups, of insiders and outsiders, of differentiation and solidarity. Miller (1971: 621*ff.*) cites an example of this process by listing a whole string of terms used by characters to address or refer to a man named Matsuo, the father of a family running a flower store in a television soap drama. These include 'company president' (*shachō*) used by a young female employee; 'bro' (*aniki*) used by his younger brother who is a partner and also employed in the store; 'chief' (*danna*) adopted by a younger male employee; 'father' (*o-tōsan*) and 'the old man' (*oyaji*)—both used by his son—one as a form of address, the other as one of reference behind his father's back; 'uncle' (*ojisan*) adopted by an unrelated younger female lodger in his house; 'elder brother' (*onīsan*) used by his sister-in-law; 'you' (*anata*), a normal form of address used by wives towards their husbands; and 'my man' (*uchi no hito*) when Matsuo's wife refers to him in his absence.

This idea of 'us' versus 'them', or rather 'those who are not us', can be found in a number of vocabulary items. There are special pairs of verbs, for example, which correspond to 'we' and 'non-we': *mōsu*, to 'speak', can only be used for oneself; *ossharu* only for somebody else speaking. *Haiken* is used when the speaker wants to 'take a look' at something; *goran* when someone else looks at it. Similarly, a very large number of nouns can be prefixed by the honorific particle *o-* or *go-*: *kao* is 'my' face; *o-kao* anybody's face except my own. It can be seen that these minutiae of linguistic usage make 'pronouns' as such virtually unnecessary.

Another obvious example of the way in which social groupings are pinpointed by language use is to be found in the differences which exist between male and female speech. These are too numerous to be cited in any great detail here, but differences include personal referents (fem. *atashi, atakushi*; masc. *boku, ore, washi*), interrogative particles (fem. *no*; masc. *ka*), verb final particles (fem. *wa, yo*; masc. *zo, na*), and lexical items such as 'eat' (fem. *taberu*; masc. *kuu*), or 'tasty' (fem. *oishii*; masc. *umai*). Besides these, there is a general tendency for men to use 'heavy' sounding Chinese compounds in their speech, while women avoid these and use the more 'Japanese' sounding *yamato kotoba*.[9]

While women clearly differentiate themselves from men in their use of linguistic forms (Ide 1982), it can also be argued that they find a sense of solidarity in their being able to use a type of language which is patently female (and not necessarily despised). This kind of in-group solidarity is also to be found in areas outside the division of the sexes. The *burakumin* 'outcasts', for instance, use a number of non-standard linguistic forms (*cf.* Wagatsuma and De Vos 1967: 374–5, 380–1), while some pop musicians use a form of reverse slang among themselves—*tāgi* for 'guitar', *sūbē* for 'bass', and *naon* for 'woman' (*onna*).[10] In each case, we can see that occupational differentiation gives rise to a special in-group code.

This willingness to create solidarity wherever possible can also be seen in the old *kuruwa kotoba* used by prostitutes, *geisha*, and other entertainers and their customers during the Edo period. This code of communication was adopted by all those visiting and employed in the night quarters, since it enabled guests to conceal their various social statuses and hostesses their low-class regional accents. This masterly stroke of linguistic genius, designed to overcome all differentiation, and to create solidarity among a motley collection of people unlikely to communicate at all under normal circumstances, has now, alas, died out.

A sense of 'Japaneseness'

In general, the most striking point about everyday speech in Japanese society is the continual process of differentiation that it exhibits. This differentiation occurs primarily at the micro-level of the family, of an occupational group, or of gender, but it can also be extended to the macro-level where it sets the whole of the Japanese race apart from the rest of the world. Thus, we find that some words, like that for 'emperor', differ according to whether they are used to refer to the Japanese emperor (*tennō*), or to the emperor of another country (*kōtei*). Similarly, Japanese ships have the suffix -*maru* added to their names, while foreign ships take the suffix -*gō*; Japanese islands are generally referred to as -*shima*, foreign islands as -*tō* (*cf.* Miller 1967: 621–2). This process of separation between 'Japanese' and 'non-Japanese' in the lexicon also extends to the written language, where the *hiragana* syllabary is used to write Japanese words, and *katakana* syllabary loan-words (imported predominantly from Western languages), and where even Chinese characters have their 'Chinese' (*on*) and 'Japanese' (*kun*) readings.

In other words, regardless of whether they are male or female, or of which of many in-groups they may belong to, there is one boundary at which all Japanese can finally draw the line of differentiation and identify. It is at this point that I wish to turn to what was earlier referred to as the 'macro-level' approach to the study of language in Japanese society, and examine the way in which language has an overall currency accepted by the whole of society. My particular concern here will be with a language of ideology, with a vocabulary of keywords which aims not at differentiation but at *solidarity* and at moulding people into an image of what it means to be 'Japanese'.

In the literature on Japanese society, scholars have used a number of words and phrases to mark out certain aspects of social or cultural significance: *giri*, or 'socially contracted dependence', is one of the more important of these, and its counterpart *ninjō*, or 'spontaneity', another. Together with this pair, Benedict (1946), for example, has discussed further concepts such as *on*, 'indebtedness', *kō*, 'duty to one's parents', and *chū*, 'duty to the Emperor', and Doi (1981) has alluded to several more terms in his exposition of *amae*, the dependence and presumption upon another's benevolence.

While it is true that a number of these concepts are very important to a notion of 'Japaneseness', as I shall discuss in the following chapters, it should be realised that all too often they are cited by foreign—and Japanese—scholars as examples of the 'uniqueness' of the language and culture they are studying (*cf.* Dale 1986: 77). For example, in her discussion of such words as *ai* ('love'), *ki-no-doku* (literally 'this poisonous feeling'), *arigatō* ('thank you'), *sumimasen* (literally 'it does not end'), and *katajikenai* ('I am gratefully insulted'), Benedict (1946: 103–7), gives her reader the impression that Japanese is full of idioms which cannot possibly be translated properly into our own language. Doi, too, in his discussion of *amae*, points out that while this feeling of 'passive love' may be found all over the world, only the Japanese have managed to give that feeling a word (1981: 28). Since he later suggests that *amae* depends on *ninjō* and that the nature of feelings expressed in *ninjō* is itself peculiar to the Japanese (*ibid.* p. 33), it will be appreciated that certain Japanese key concepts are being used to set Japan as a nation apart from the rest of the world.

Every nation has its myths, of course, and the Japanese are in this respect no exception to the rule. The myth in this case is the Japanese language, which is seen to be 'unique', 'special' and 'distinctive' (and by extension so are its speakers—or, at least, those of them who possess a Japanese passport). Miller (1982: 32) argues that the Japanese language is the 'major sustaining myth of Japanese society' and that it reinforces the questions posed by those concerned with propagating the uniqueness of Japanese culture: 'Who are we? Where did we come from? Where are we going?' My own argument is that popular cultural forms use language to support the myth of Japaneseness, as well as to reinforce some internal social divisions—particularly between young and old, and women and men—on the one hand, while denying others such as class, on the other. Just how this is done will be seen in the following chapters.

Notes

1 In that the Japanese frequently use their language as a focal point of identity, and thereby as a means of setting themselves apart from all other linguistic and cultural groups, it would seem that they are prepared to accept the stronger version of the Sapir–Whorf hypothesis: that a people's perceptions of the world are determined by the structure of the language they speak (*cf.* Whorf 1956: 212–14). Such 'myths' put forward by the Japanese about their language have recently been criticised by Miller (1982) and Dale (1986), both of whom have launched venomous, and at times hilarious, attacks on this aspect of *nihonjin-ron*, or 'the cult of being Japanese'. Incidentally, I would like to take this opportunity to thank Peter Dale for providing me with the splendid example of T shirt English with which this book opens.

2 Much of what follows is based on Martin 1964; Miller 1967, chapter 7; and Miller 1971.

3 I follow Haugen who takes issue with Friedrich (in Bright 1966) for referring to pronominal usage as part of the *grammatical* structure of (in this case the Russian) language, and who suggests that we are here talking about *lexical* facts.

4 Much of the discussion of the Japanese honorific system below is paralleled—if Geertz (1972: 167–79) is to be believed—in Javanese speech behaviour. Martin (1964) also compares Japanese with Korean.

5 This supports Nakane's observation (1970: 32) that ranking is determined by status first, then age, then sex.

6 For further discussion of speech levels, status and conflict in a television 'home drama' see Niyekawa 1984 (especially pp. 75–78).

7 A prime example of such competitiveness and opposition is to be found in political factionalism (see, e.g., Baerwald 1979).

8 The overall coherence of these orientational metaphors suggests that what is good is *ura* and *uchi*, rather than *omote* and *soto*, and thus contradicts some of the conclusions drawn by Lakoff and Johnson (1980, esp. pp. 17–19).

9 *Yamato kotoba* can perhaps best be defined as what remains of the Japanese language after all foreign words—particularly Chinese compounds—have been removed therefrom.

10 This type of reverse slang, or syllabic exchange, is mentioned by Loveday (1986: 305) in the context of the underworld's argot.

Wine, language and song

Introduction

So much for a broad view of the way in which language usage reflects, or points to, certain features of Japanese society. But I want to continue this microlevel approach by looking more closely at two features mentioned in the previous chapter: solidarity and differentiation, on the one hand, and the distinction between *tatemae* and *honne*, on the other. To do this, I am going to look at one version of the 'Japanese wine ceremony'—*sake* drinking in a small pottery community in the southern island of Kyushu.

Anyone who spends any length of time in Japan soon discovers that drinking is an indispensable social activity. Certainly there is a whole set of cultural forms that accompany the imbibation of alcohol—from Japanese dancing by (self-styled) *geisha* to popular ballads, together with all the technological wizardry that surrounds their reproduction. It is almost as if two worlds exist side by side in Japan's cities—one with its department stores and office blocks, peopled by housewives and 'salarymen'; the other with its less permanent buildings in which these same businessmen carouse away the hours of darkness, hoarsely singing to the strains of the *karaoke* ('empty orchestra') machine, and soothed by the murmured sweet nothings and occasional caresses of attractive hostesses who pour their drinks. There is a world of light and a world of darkness (known as *mizu shōbai*, or the 'water trade' (see Morley 1985)), the Siamese twins of Japanese industrial capitalism. Foreign businessmen recount (often not without a trace of nostalgia) tales of how they have been taken to expensive bars by their Japanese hosts and of how it is in the friendly, informal and sexually suggestive atmosphere of these bars that they have been able to conclude many a business deal.[1]

When I went to do fieldwork for the first time in Sarayama, a community of potters in Kyushu, I soon discovered that people drink more seriously in the country than they do, perhaps, in cities. As a newcomer to a rural community, I was feted at first almost every night as the local inhabitants began checking out my weaknesses. Could I hold my liquor? Was I able to sing and dance? Was I really what I pretended to be—an anthropologist— or was I, perhaps, a government spy or local tax inspector in disguise? Above all, was I a good drinking companion?

Before describing these drinking sessions, I ought to make two points about a person's supposed behaviour while 'under the influence'. It has often been suggested that, in Japan, what is said during the course of a drinking session is soon forgiven and forgotten. Drinking acts as an outlet for repressed feelings, goes the argument—feelings that are repressed mainly because of the tension between individual desires and group pressures in Japanese society. It is only while drinking that a junior may forcefully criticise a senior to his (or possibly her) face, and only while drinking that a senior will accept such open criticism. Drinking is seen to break down all social barriers. It provides a 'frame' for egalitarian relations which nicely counterbalances the hierarchy of everyday life.

In the valley in which I lived and studied for four years between 1977 and 1982, I soon discovered that this was *not* exactly the case. Of course, people occasionally *said* that it did not matter what you told them while you were yourself under the influence of drink, but this was just an ideology designed to pull the wool over the eyes of an unsuspecting anthropologist. In fact, local residents not only remembered what was said during drinking sessions; they stored this information away, to use for their own political ends. Nothing was forgotten, since anything said under the influence of alcohol might, at some time or other, prove useful to people involved in the competitive reality of community life.

This disparity between ideals and reality became more obvious when I considered the way in which people would speak to one another while drinking together. As I pointed out in the previous chapter, the Japanese generally make a vital distinction between what they call *tatemae* and *honne*. *Tatemae* refers to the language which is used in public as a matter of 'principle'; *honne* to words that 'come from the heart' and express an individual's innermost, private feelings. It is this distinction which ultimately clarifies the relationship between group and individual in Japanese society (a relationship to which I shall have occasion to return in other contexts), for *tatemae* is the language of out-group, and *honne* that of in-group, communication.

I soon discovered that it was during drinking sessions that my informants shifted from *tatemae* to *honne*, from—to use Bernstein's distinction (1971)—'public' to 'private' language. There appeared to be no taboos concerning subject-matter and, as the evenings wore on and the *sake* flowed faster, so I found myself listening to men talking about subjects which, during daylight hours, they had either refused to discuss or had evaded with an embarrassed laugh. At the same time, I discovered that some of the answers which I had received during the normal course of interviews were directly contradicted by these same informants as we drank together. As a result, I soon found myself paying frequent visits to the lavatory so that I could jot down in my notebook revelations which oncoming alcoholic inebriation threatened to—and sometimes did—erase.

The pottery community of Sarayama

Sarayama is a small community (*buraku*) of fourteen households, of which ten make and fire a form of stoneware pottery known as *Ontayaki*, on Onta ware. Situated at the top of a narrow valley in the mountains to the north-west of the town of Hita, in central Kyushu, the community has become famous over the past three decades for a style of pottery which closely accords with the ideals of *mingei*, or folk craft, put forward by a scholar-critic, Yanagi Muneyoshi, from the late 1920s (see Chapter 5). Sarayama's potters have been praised in particular because they have steadfastly kept to traditional techniques of production—digging their own clay and glaze materials locally, using kick wheels to throw their functional wares, decorating the finished forms with certain old Korean techniques, and firing their pots in a wood-fired co-operative climbing kiln. In 1975, these techniques were designated an Intangible Cultural Property (*mukei bunkazai*) by the Japanese government's Agency for Cultural Affairs (*Bunkachō*).

Sarayama's fourteen households consist of four name groups (Kurogi, Yanase, Sakamoto and Kobukuro) and are organised along the customary lines of main-house/branch-house relations. Cross-cutting ties between name groups have been established through marriage, residential and co-operative labour groupings, together with a seniority system of age-grades whereby the oldest men have generally been in charge of community affairs (see Moeran 1984).

Until approximately 1960, there was little demand for Onta ware; the potters were primarily farmers who turned to pottery in their spare time or when the weather was too bad for them to work in the fields. In the 1960s, however, there began what came to be called the 'folk craft boom' (*mingei būmu*). Potters found that, for the first time ever, they could sell whatever they made. This increase in market demand happened to coincide with a government policy curtailing the production of rice (*gentan sei-saku*) and, during the next fifteen years, potting households began one by one to give up farming entirely. By 1979, ten of Sarayama's households were specialising full-time in pottery production, while the other four pursued such occupations as carpentry, plastering, rice farming, the cultivation of oak mushrooms (*shiitake*), running a noodle-shop, a *sake* shop and a family inn (*minshuku*).

Occupational specialisation has been accompanied by a considerable disparity of incomes between potting and non-potting households. Prior to the folk craft boom there was not that great a difference in the incomes of all households in Sarayama. Because they shared a co-operative kiln, potters fired and marketed approximately the same number of pots and earned more or less the same amount of money from them. Twenty years later, however, potting households were earning on average almost twice as much as non-potting households (¥8 million as opposed to ¥4 million). This disparity was accompanied by an ever-widening income gap among potting households, for increased demand led to some potters leaving the co-operative kiln and setting up private kilns which they could fire as and when they pleased (household incomes ranged from ¥16 to ¥5½ million in 1979).

Every rural Japanese community is ideally organised in such a way that the individual subordinates his or her interests to those of the household to which s/he belongs, and each household its interests to those of the community as a whole. A set of historical incidents has led to the Japanese rural community forming a closed social group whose inhabitants tend to see the outside world as starting a few hundred yards down the road. Sarayama is no exception to this ideal, but the recent development of the Japanese market economy has led to a number of strains in the residents' notion of community solidarity. In particular, we find that the hitherto accepted division between elders and younger men is being challenged, while the emerging economic differentiation between potting and non-potting households has further upset the much-valued emphasis placed on harmony. It is when Sarayama's men start drinking that these strains tend to break out into the open. At the same time, it is through drinking that they try to patch up their differences and recreate a feeling of 'togetherness'.

Sake-drinking parties

Drinking in Sarayama occurs on any number of pretexts and may in some exceptional circumstances start from as early as 9 o'clock in the morning. A pottery dealer, for example, may visit a potter's workshop after a kiln firing and be invited into the house for 'refreshments' at the conclusion of business. Alternatively, a forester from a nearby hamlet may drop by on his way home from work and invite one of Sarayama's inhabitants down to the local *sake* shop for a few bottles of beer. A potter may have to discuss firing schedules with other potters sharing the cooperative kiln, and they may decide to share a few drinks together at the home of one of the potters, in the community noodle-shop, or even down in one of the bars of the local town, 17 kilometres away. Here, however, I wish to discuss formal drinking encounters, when either the community as a whole, or the ten households forming the potters' co-operative, gather together to celebrate Sarayama's ceremonial occasions. Some of these ceremonies involve fixed amounts of *sake*: the Mountain God festival (*Yama no kami*), for example, is limited to one *gō* (0.18 litres) of *sweet sake* (*amazake*) per household; on New Year's Day, only one *shō* (1.8 litres) of *sake* is drunk at the villagers' annual greeting. Most ceremonies, however, do not limit the amount of alcohol to be consumed, and it is these which I shall discuss here.

Such ceremonial occasions tend to follow a general pattern. Community gatherings rotate among households and are usually attended by one man (and sometimes one woman) from each household in Sarayama, the time of day being announced over the community's loudspeaker system. Special ceremonies, such as the potters' celebration of *Ebisu-sama* (God of Trade), held only once a year, are initiated by the sound of a conch shell, blown by the 'duty officer' (*sewa motokata*), whose job it is to look after community affairs for the year. At the appointed hour, representatives from each household gather at the place where the ceremony is to be held. On arriving, each representative takes off his shoes and steps up into the hallway, before making his way to the *nando*, or *kotatsu* room, an informal living-room where the household's family gathers to eat, socialise and watch television. There he will be served green tea and be asked to help himself from a tray of candies or bowl of fruit. Idle conversation will ensue, centring mainly on the host's family, with comments on how big the children are growing, how well they are getting on at school, and so on. The emphasis here is on household members, or on events occurring in the outside world. Community affairs as such are not discussed.[3]

Once everyone is assembled, the host will ask people to move into the main guest room (*zashiki*), where low tables have been laid out in an inverted U-shape. The *zashiki* in fact often comprises two rooms, separated by sliding screens which can be removed when many visitors are present. Tables are lined down each side of these rooms as well as across the top. I say 'down' and 'top' and 'inverted' U-shape for a reason. Behind the lateral row of tables is to be found the *tokonoma*, a slightly raised 'sacred dais' which is built into every country house. The *tokonoma* is considered to be the most important part of the whole building and so only the most important people are placed with their backs to it along the top row of tables. In the event of casual visiting, a guest will always be placed with his back to the *tokonoma*, while the host will sit opposite him in an inferior position. On community occasions, the eldest household representative present is placed at the centre of the top table, the second eldest is placed to his right, the third to his left, the fourth to the second eldest's right, and so on right down the two lines of tables to the most junior men present. When women participate, they are placed below the men and adopt a similar order of seating by seniority. Younger women, however, seem to be less particular about the seating order and occasionally younger housewives find themselves 'above' somebody who is their senior by a year or so. In general, it can be said that the older a man or woman becomes, the more strictly he or she adheres to seating by age seniority, and that men tend to be stricter than women about seating order.

Once everyone is settled and kneeling formally in front of his place (each place being marked by a side saucer, chopsticks and empty *sake* cup, together with a small covered lacquer bowl of clear fish soup, a porcelain bowl of boiled vegetables or *niimono* and a side dish of raw fish), the host, who is not included in the age seniority seating order but kneels at the bottom of the room, formally greets and welcomes his guests. The most senior member of those present then replies in a speech which is highly formalised, consisting of a number of set phrases thanking everyone for taking the trouble to gather together at such a busy time, and praising the elements for being so kind as to favour the occasion with good weather (this bit may be dropped when the weather is not so benign, or substituted by comments on how people must be suffering from the cold, snow, rain, wind, or whatever).

Having made these initial comments in reply to the host's greeting, the eldest man proceeds to blur the in-group/out-group distinction hitherto present by informing everyone about why they have gathered together on this particular occasion. The rarer the occasion, the more detailed this information is likely to be and the more the occasion stressed. The host household will then be thanked for providing a place for everyone to gather. Everyone is thanked again for taking the trouble to come, and a toast is proposed. At this point, the women will get up and move away from their places at the bottom of the room to fill everyone's *sake* cup from the bottles of heated alcohol that stand already on the tables. The speaker raises his voice: '*Kanpai!*' (Glasses dry!')—or, on less formal occasions, '*itadakimasu*' ('for what we humbly receive'). The cry is taken up by all present as they, too, raise their cups and drink. For a few seconds there is silence as everyone drinks together. The contents of each cup are downed. There is a sudden exhalation of breath as people express their satisfaction with the *sake*.

This marks the end of the initial stage of the ceremonial gathering, and participants now find themselves slipping into informality as they shift from a kneeling to a cross-legged position and refill their cups. They will start sipping soup and eating some of the food spread before them, but not too much, for drinking is the important activity and it is a man's capacity to drink and talk which in the end marks him out from among his fellows. The first cup or two of *sake* is poured out for him by those sitting on either side and he in turn will fill his neighbours' cups, since it is considered impolite to serve oneself. Frequently, the women will remain on the inner side of the inverted U-shape of tables and serve the men with rice wine as they join in the casual conversation. This starts with somewhat formalised exclamations on the weather, food and other people's business, before shifting to more informal gossip and a discussion of recent community events. It is at this stage that a man proceeds to exchange cups with his neighbours.

What does an exchange of *sake* cups consist of?[4] When his cup is empty, a man will pick it up and, holding it by the foot rim balanced between the tips of his fingers, he will present it to someone sitting nearby. As he presents the cup, he will call the other person's name and raise the hand with which he is holding the cup very slightly once or twice, in order to attract the other person's attention. This gesture is at the same time a sign of humility from a man offering a gift. The receiver will take the cup—usually with an exclamation of slightly feigned surprise—bow his head slightly, again raise the cup in his hand in a gesture of humble acceptance, and allow the donor to fill it for him from one of the bottles on the table between them. The receiver then downs the *sake* and almost immediately returns the cup with a similar set of formal expressions and gestures.

When a man exchanges cups with his immediate neighbours, the flow of conversation is not immediately affected in any appreciable way. However, the first exchange is a signal for those concerned to shift from informal gossip to somewhat more intimate conversation about how events, previously touched upon, affect those concerned. When a man has exchanged cups with those sitting immediately next to him, he will proceed to pass cups to others sitting further away. Each time, the same formalities are gone through, but here the purpose of the exchanges is for the donor to take the opportunity to initiate a conversation with someone else (or, possibly, to draw him into a continuing conversation). A man may well have to go through a preliminary round of formal pleasantries but will, with a second exchange of cups with the same person, proceed to informal and more intimate conversation.

Provided that the people with whom he is exchanging cups are within arm's reach, a man will tend to remain seated in his initial position according to age. However, as the gathering gains a certain alcoholic momentum, men will find themselves exchanging cups with others several feet away, since it is considered rude to drink on one's own without exchanging cups and since every man wants to spread and reinforce his web of contacts as widely as possible. In this case, a man may have to pass a cup along the table via his neighbours; or he may prefer to get up and walk along behind where everyone is sitting in order to exchange cups. Sometimes, he may step across the low table in front of him into the middle of the room and proceed to exchange cups with a fellow drinker from the inside of the inverted U-shape (previously occupied only by the women). This point in the cup exchanges can be said to mark the third stage of the ceremonial gathering, and it is usually by this time that the women will have withdrawn to talk, drink and eat among themselves at the bottom of the room.

This third stage usually begins within ten to fifteen minutes after the proposal of the formal toast, and it is from this time that the gathering starts to become a 'serious' drinking session. It is marked by complete informality of speech, with virtually no restrictions on who says what to whom. Whereas the initial formal opening was probably conducted in standard Japanese (or as closely approximating the standard as local elders can manage), both the second and third stages are characterised by use of dialect. Potters and other residents of Sarayama speak in their own language, not in some idiom imposed on them by ephemeral outsiders in Tokyo or wherever.

It is said that in the past (a vague term which can refer to any time between ten and fifty years previously, depending on the speaker's age), a man could exchange *sake* cups only with someone sitting below him. He was strictly prohibited from passing his cup up the table to anyone older than himself (*cf*. Befu 1974: 200). This meant that, to some extent, the shift from the second to the third stage of the gathering was determined by the elders, since it was they who made the first move in getting up to exchange cups with others junior to them who were sitting out of arm's reach lower down the tables. It was, of course, possible for a certain amount of lateral movement to occur, since people of very similar ages found themselves on opposite sides of the room as a result of formal seating arrangements, and they were permitted to cross over to exchange cups with one another. Nowadays, however, it is possible for a man to pass his cup 'up' the table to someone his senior, although it would still be slightly presumptuous for a man of—say—thirty to exchange cups with his neighbours and then step across the table, walk up to the top of the room and present his *sake* cup to one of the elders at the top table. He would be expected first to present cups to at least one or two of the older men sitting between him and those at the top. Once the third stage has begun, however, and has been continuing for five or ten minutes, a young person can suddenly break away from his drinking group and walk straight up to the top of the tables to exchange cups with men there. The breakdown of formality permits this. At the same time, many of the oldest men will have 'come down' to sit in the middle of the room, so that a younger person can join and exchange cups with an elder much more unobtrusively by first presenting his cup to—say—a forty-year-old man and talking with him (although codes of politeness presuppose an elder to be accorded first cup when he is talking in a small group).

I have used the word 'unobtrusively' here for a reason. People do not just exchange cups during these drinking sessions; they talk. And they do not talk just about local gossip and other trivia. As the *sake* flows, they tend to talk about those affairs which are closest to their hearts and which rankle in their minds. Hence, conversation is political in the context of the community, and a man is constantly alert during the course of drinking, weighing up who is talking to whom, putting two and two together from his background knowledge of local affairs, and frequently using the custom of cup exchanges to join a conversation in which he feels that he might well have a vested interest. To a certain extent, those who really wish to make use of the gathering to further their intra-community political interests will do their best to move about unobtrusively and to make their membership of certain drinking groups seem as casual as possible. They will decide what they want to talk about and who the best person would be to talk over the matter. They then proceed to plan a route towards drinking with that person in as 'natural' a manner as possible, so that when they do meet, their conversation will not attract the attention of others. This may prove difficult, especially when both men concerned are moving about the room independently, per-haps with completely different strategies, but during the course of the third stage (which can last for an hour or more) they are bound to get together sometime and the matter in hand will be discussed. There are, after all, only fourteen households in the community and, even when both father and son attend a drinking session, there are rarely more than twenty-five men present at any gathering.

As I mentioned earlier, so far as the formal organisation of Sara-yama is concerned, it is the elders who officially hold the reins of authority in the community. It is the men over sixty years of age whose opinions are publicly respected and whose commands are generally obeyed. These men still remain heads of their house-holds, even though they may have sons living and working with them who are in their mid-thirties and in the prime of life so far as their physical strength is concerned. The point of interest about drinking sessions, therefore, is that when the third informal stage is reached, it is not the elders but the middle-aged men who are the most active in the exchange of *sake* cups. The first to get up from their seats and move about the room are almost invariably younger heads of households, aged between forty and sixty. Some men are slower to get up than others, perhaps, but in the end it is the middle-aged group of men who are talking, arguing and con-suming the most *sake*. The oldest men remain more or less rooted to the top tables with their temporary visitors seated before them.

In the meantime, potters up to their mid-thirties generally form their own drinking groups at the far end of the room, very often sitting with the women. This means that the centre of the *zashiki* becomes completely empty, so that the third stage in the drinking session is marked by a complete separation of participants into two groups. Those at the bottom of the room keep their conversation light and trivial; they discuss such things as local and professional baseball games, fishing, popular music and their occasional outings to bars in Hita (and appraise the hostesses working there). Those at the top of the room generally discuss community affairs, local valley politics, problems surrounding Sarayama's pottery production and other matters seen to be important for the community as a whole (see Figures 1, 2 and 3).

By this time the women will have begun clearing some of the unoccupied tables of dishes, and use kitchen work as an excuse to retire from the main room to the back of the house (where they indulge just as earnestly in their own gossip and political manoeuvring). A number of men will be getting very drunk. (The only thing that prevents them from getting drunk sooner is the fact that they are provided with large ashtrays, into which a man will tip out much of the *sake* poured for him when his interlocutor is not looking. Although frowned upon by those who can hold their drink, this 'bad' habit is generally accepted since complete drunkenness is not thought to be conducive to a good party.) There is a tendency at this point for many of the eldest men to retire quietly (frequently by way of the lavatory) to the *kotatsu* room. There they will sit and watch television over a cup of tea, talking once more in restrained voices about the nothing-in-particulars of life in a country valley. One of their peers or juniors may stagger in and make an attempt to drag them back into the main room and then use their refusal as an excuse for himself to stay in the *kotatsu* room and drop out of the drinking. It is generally at this point that the gathering enters its fourth stage.

This stage is marked, then, by the departure of the elders and by the introduction of singing, and sometimes dancing. Singing is important, for it enables one man to claim the attention of others. This means two things: not only do men break off their conversa-

Key	Households	Potting		Non-potting	
1–4 = 60+ years		Kaneichi	1, 19	Yamamaru	2, 9
5–7 = 50+ ..		Yamani	3, 14	Kaneyo	18
8–11 = 40+ ..		Yamasai	15	Maruta	8
12–16 = 30+ ...		Irisai	10	Yamamasu	16
17–21 = 20+ ..		Kanemaru	7, 21		
		Yamasan	6, 20		
x = women		Irisan	5, 13		
		Yamaichi	11		
		Iriichi	12		
		Yamako	4, 17		

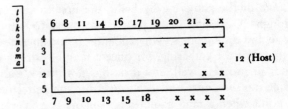

Figure 1: Formal Seating Arrangement (Stage 1)

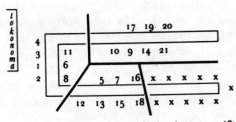

Figure 2: Informal Seating Arrangement (Stage 2)

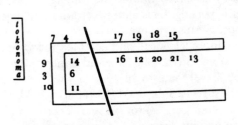

Figure 3: Informal Seating Arrangement (Stage 3)

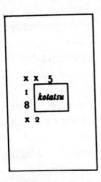

29

tions in order to listen to one man singing, but a man's ability to attract attention by standing up and singing may well stand him in good stead later on during his own political arguments with others. Singing in itself livens up the party. A successful singer will find himself at the centre of attention, and he may well be able to turn this attention into support in order to help him present, and win, an argument at a later stage when a quarrel breaks out.

In general, people tend to listen to the first songs that are sung, but to ignore later singers and continue their conversations uninterrupted. This means that it is to one's own advantage to initiate the fourth stage of the gathering by being the first to sing. The problem, though, is gauging when people are likely to want to listen to a song and timing one's own exuberation to coincide with the general mood of the gathering, for once a man has drunk too much he tends not to sing well, and if he has not drunk enough he may well be too self-conscious to put over his song effectively. The precise point when a man gambles on singing is a matter of delicate political finesse. Sometimes someone will suddenly decide to start siging, raise his voice in the hope of catching the attention of everyone present, and find that in fact people are not yet ready for a song and ignore him entirely. The man who can stand up, claim the attention of one and all in a loud voice, and then keep that attention focused on himself right to the end of his song, is also likely to be able to claim their attention when it comes to arguing community affairs. An effective singing voice is in some respects essential to winning an argument, and winning an argument is the prerequisite for a community leader.

Here we should note that it is the men in the middle age-group, and not the elders, who generally initiate the singing successfully. If a younger man starts singing, he is almost certain to be ignored. This is partly, perhaps, because younger men tend to sing popular songs, rather than the more 'classical' and accepted forms of *utai*, *shigin* or *minyō* folk-songs favoured by the older men. Men from the middle age-group have come to be known for their singing prowess: Shigeki (11) for his Shimazaki Tōson songs, Moriyuki (9) for his *minyō*, and Toshiyasu (7) for his *utai*. Those who want to get ahead in community life have a tendency to perfect a certain style of singing which is acceptable to, and praised by, other villagers.

As the singing gathers atonal momentum, so conversations

30

among drinkers become more earnest. Men will by now have
downed their quota of seven gō of sake (the amount considered
equivalent to our eight pints of beer), and their speech will be
slurred as they no longer hold back on topics which they hold
most dear to their hearts. One potter will accuse another of selling
his tea bowls at five times the agreed retail price; another will
upbraid a neighbour for maltreating his daughter-in-law and forc-
ing her back to work immediately after a miscarriage; a group
of potters will get at one of their number who has arbitrarily had
a woodshed built on a piece of land over which the bulldozer must
pass to dig out all the potters' clay. It is at this point that major
arguments, quarrels, even fights occur. Almost invariably, it is
those in the middle age-group (nos. 5 to 11 in the Figures) who
are the most voluble, particularly potters, who are jostling for
position as next leader of the co-operative and hence, in time, of
the community as a whole. Frequently they fight amongst themselves and it is the junior age-groups or those who (like 9) are not
potters who act as intermediaries and try to stop the men concerned from coming to blows.[5]

It is about this time that most men make up their minds about
whether they are really going to make a night of it, or whether
they will slip away. Younger men in particular tend to leave now,
and soon there is only a handful of men left in the zashiki. By
common consent, they may all move to the kotatsu room, where
they will continue to drink sake, or turn to tea. One or two men
who, like the dormouse at Alice's tea party, have fallen asleep,
may well be roused and made to join in what is left of the party.
This is the fifth and final stage of the drinking session, and can be
marked by more anger and quarrelling, or by a general sobering
up of all concerned. Sometimes, when everyone is feeling in a
particularly good mood, someone will telephone for a taxi and the
men will go down to Hita for further, more expensive, frolicking
in the town's bars.

Conclusion

I have shown here that sake-drinking parties in the community of
Sarayama follow much the same pattern as that described for
drinking among the Subanun (see Frake 1964). Drinking sessions

Table 1   *Analysis of Drinking Parties*

Encounter stages	Discourse stages	Focus of speech acts	Language type
1 Formal gathering	Formal opening speech and toast	Role expression	Standard
2 Immobile cup exchange	Semi-formal introductory talk	Context definition	Dialect
	Local gossip; intimate level discussion	Topic (household)	Dialect
3 Mobile cup exchange	Intimate level discussion	Topic (community affairs)	Dialect
4 Song drinking	Singing as verbal art;	Stylistic	Dialect/Standard
	Discussions and quarrels	Topic (community affairs)	Dialect
5 Informal separation	Incoherence (?)	Context closure	Dialect

can be divided into five discourse stages, each of which has a separate focus of speech act and separate language-type (see Table 1). Among both the Subanun and the residents of Sarayama, drinking talk takes on importance in the context of the assumption of authority. Among the Subanun, verbal skills during drinking encounters enable a man to act as legislator in disputes and thereby to gain status in the eyes of his fellow men. Among the potters of Sarayama, the ability to talk and sing well ensures a man a position of power in community affairs. The more mobile a man and the better able he is to talk to all, the more likely he is to assume authority. Drinking is thus a political activity.

The point to be made about the community of Sarayama is that drinking encounters would appear to reflect the growing loss of power of the elders and the increasing influence of the middle-aged group of men in community affairs. What should be stressed here is that, although on *formal* occasions the eldest men assume authority through formal speeches and through such overt marks of deference as being seated at the head of the table at drinking parties, *in*formally it is the group of men below them who wield most power. It is those between the ages of forty and sixty who manipulate to their own ends the conversations which occur during drinking sessions, and who argue out vital community matters. I would suggest that it is this middle age-group—in particular two or three articulate men—who covertly influence formal decisions overtly made by the elders. The loss of power of the latter can be seen in the fact that, firstly, the elders no longer determine the overall pattern of a drinking encounter, because they no longer have the prerogative to dictate the course of *sake* cup exchanges; and secondly, the elders cannot sing well and tend to remove themselves somewhat rapidly from major drinking encounters, leaving their immediate juniors to discuss and virtually to decide important community matters. Elders retain their authority in official *ex cathedra* statements, but in practice these comments are influenced by those junior to them.

Of course, it could be argued that the elders are able to leave *sake* parties early precisely because their sons are often present as well. They remain secure in the knowledge that information will be relayed to them from a trustworthy source. The trouble with this argument is that there are several drinking encounters where only *one* member from each household is present and yet the elders still leave early. In such cases, there is no guarantee that they will learn, let alone be able to influence indirectly, what happens in their absence.

Another criticism might take the line that, in fact, it is *usually* the middle-aged who are the most influential in any small-scale society, and that the notion that the elders used to be in control of community matters is a typical idealisation of a state of affairs which has never in fact existed. This is possible. After all, the elders have never been able to sing well, so did they leave drinking sessions early in the past? I cannot be sure about this, of course, but potters in Sarayama used to stress that in the past the main activity of the elders was drinking (*hikari*) and that they would frequently gather over a few bottles of home-made *sake* and come to decisions about community affairs without bothering to consult the younger household heads. It is claimed that one reason for this was that younger men were too busy farming to be able to get together very much. It is here, perhaps, that the farmers' conversion to full-time pottery may have affected drinking habits, for the middle age-group of men are now always at home in their workshops, rather than scattered in distant fields up to three kilometres from Sarayama, and can gather at a few minutes' notice. Not only this, but the development of a market for folk-craft pottery, together with the emergence of a notion of 'artistic talent' as a result of the external criticism of Onta ware, has enabled younger potters to have more say in the running of the potters' co-operative.[6] All in all, therefore, it would seem that the pattern of drinking parties described here reflects fairly the general pattern of the erosion of the power of the elders over the past quarter of a century.

A second point to be made in this connection is that drinking *per se* is not what really counts. By this I mean that it does not matter if a man is too old, or not physically strong enough, to hold his alcohol. Provided that he is prepared to stay with his drinking companions and not go home early, a man can still wield a lot of influence. In other words, drinking in itself is a desirable, but not essential, prerequisite for power. This point is best illustrated by one potter, Shigeki (11), who at one stage during fieldwork was suffering from a bad liver and had been advised by his doctor to stop drinking *sake* for a few months. This he did. But rather than delegate his wife or even son to go along to community *sake* parties, Shigeki himself attended them (complete with a supply of tomato juice). Not only this, but he used to stay until the fifth and final stage of almost every drinking session, and so participated in all the major discussions that took place. He even went so far as to feign a certain drunkenness and exclaim that tomato juice made him 'happy' because he drank it out of used *sake* cups. What I wish to stress is that Shigeki had no need to attend these gatherings in the first place; alternatively, he could have put in an appearance and left early at about the third stage (this is precisely what another man from a non-potting household, Osamu (8), who complained of a bad liver, used to do—a fact which illustrates, I think, the way in which potters are more concerned with power than are non-potters). The fact that Shigeki chose to remain to the bitter end shows the importance he attached to the way in which community affairs were discussed during these gatherings. To have missed them would have meant a considerable weakening of his own position of power within the community. Drinking is thus the idiom in which decisions are made, and not necessarily their cause.

Which brings me back to my original point about drinking acting as a licensed outlet for repressed frustration. When insulted on such an occasion, a man is supposed to behave the next day as if nothing had happened. All is forgiven and forgotten, it is said. But to suggest this is, in my opinion, to take an extremely naive view of Japanese (or indeed any) society. It is clear from my fieldwork in Sarayama that people were offended by quarrels picked during the course of drinking sessions and that, although they did their best to pretend that they had not been offended, the old adage that what is said under the influence of alcohol is always forgotten was simply not true. I soon learned that people in Sarayama, even people who appeared at the time to be very drunk, remembered very clearly who had said what to whom and why during parties. Not only this, but these discussions and disputes, which were not openly discussed during the course of everyday activities, were weighed and *used* in further arguments. Drinking arguments thus formed a covert discourse which people proceeded to draw on for the advance of their own political interests. There were, in other words, two discourses in action in Sarayama. One was the overt daytime discourse, conducted mainly by the elders and in fairly formal situations. The other was a covert night-time discourse entered into by the middle-aged group of men, mainly under the informal influence of *sake*. It was vital for any man who wished to gain access to authority and power to be aware of the night-time discourse and to make use of it as and when appropriate. In other words, if he was to gain any position of authority in the community, a man was bound to drink, or at least keep company with drinkers.

Much of the discussion of drinking parties in Sarayama ties in with work done on political oratory in traditional societies. The way in which potters use informal occasions such as those described here to hammer out community problems is paralleled, for example, by the Maori in New Zealand, who make use of informal meetings to decide local and inter-tribal matters. In each of the two societies we find that some questions are perennial

35

favourites for debate—the arguments about the production, marketing and aesthetic appraisal of Onta ware in Sarayama, the teaching of the Maori language and preservation of Maori culture in New Zealand *marae*—and also that these questions are never really settled, *because none of the participants wants to settle them*. We find, too, that the distinction between *tatemae* and *honne* is similar to the distinction made by Salmond (1975: 62–3) between 'tight' oratory and 'loose' plain speaking, and to that made by Rosaldo (1973) between 'crooked' and 'straight' speech. Indeed, it ties in with the more generalised distinction made by Bloch (1975: 13) between 'formalised' and 'everyday' speech.

Bloch's notion that there is a correlation to be made between types of political oratory and types of political system has been reformulated by Borgstrom (1982), who suggests that the mode of political address correlates with the type of power relationship pertaining between speaker and audience. In general, types of speech have been seen to reflect power relations between superior and inferior, and in this respect, perhaps, *tatemae* and *honne* are not so different. But they also encompass a second, frequently perceived distinction between *omote*, the 'open' where surprises should not occur, and *ura*, the 'back' which shrouds the wheeling and dealing which lead up to decision making (see Johnson 1980). What goes on in the Japanese Diet, for example, is *omote*; the real political bargaining amongst factions is all *ura*. This makes oratory as such unnecessary.

The fact that *tatemae* is linked to *omote* also ties in with the Japanese sociological idea, already mentioned, that the individual should subordinate his or her interests to those of the group, for *tatemae* is the expression of group ideology. In this respect, then, it is not simply a form of 'authority' speech, but a means by which an in-group shuts itself off from the outside world. *Tatemae* and *honne* represent both authority and power, public and private, politeness and intimacy, form and content, out-group and in-group. In other words, Japanese data suggest that we should not interpret relations of authority and power only in terms of a hierarchical structure, but also as a function of social distance (*cf.* politeness forms and Bernstein's restricted and elaborated codes) which extends *horizontally* between in-groups and out-groups.

This is an important point, firstly because it is often missed by those who see the Japanese as operating *only* in the sphere of vertical relations; secondly, because one of the aims of those who preside over the production of popular culture in general would seem to be to deny the existence of social distance. The reasoning here is splendidly circular, but extremely effective. If *manga* comics, for example, *are* seen to be available to *everyone*—retired bureaucrat or college student, golfing husband or culture vulture wife, urbane professional or country farmer—their underlying ideals will not be questioned. But precisely because such ideology remains unquestioned, comics will be seen to be available to all. This is the real success of most popular cultural forms (*cf.* Schodt 1983: 150). Starting out on the periphery, they are quickly made central to the workings of Japanese society. The underlying message is simple: life may have its fair share of ups and downs, but we also need a certain amount of equilibrium if we are to survive!

Notes

1 For those who might think Japan to the somehow special in this regard, let me quote Sir William Harcourt's words of 1872: 'As much of the history of England has been brought about in public ale-houses as in the House of Commons.'

2 It would, perhaps, be tempting providence to declare that the whole of my Ph.D. thesis (and the book which derived from it) were written on the basis of information given under the benign influence of *sake*. I would, however, be attempting to delude all and sundry were I to suggest that I could have begun to write a thesis without participating regularly in the *sake* parties held so frequently in Sarayama. Those interested in the general topic of anthropologists doing fieldwork might like to glance at my *Ōkubo Diary: Portrait of a Japanese Valley* (Stanford University Press 1985).

3 This format of conversational niceties is, of course, not limited to a remote Japanese valley community. I have noticed that English suburban dinner parties tend to go through a similar shift in conversational style as guests proceed from cocktails to food.

4 Harumi Befu has recently brought to my attention an article which he published in *Arctic Anthropology* on after-dinner entertainment in general. In this he outlines a number of 'elementary rules of the *sake* party' which are mentioned here, and talks of the 'socially defined rules of drunken behavior'. Although I read much of this article with a certain sense of *déjà vu*, I feel that my own work retains some value for its analysis of a specific ethnographic community.

5 It should be pointed out here that there are some songs which are consciously

sung in order to avoid or stifle quarrels and that these are folk songs, like the *Tankō bushi* or *Kuroda bushi*, which immediately create a sense of community and harmony. It is not surprising, therefore, to find that it is frequently the man who is good at singing these folk songs (Moriyuki (9)) who acts as mediator in arguments which get out of control.

6 I have discussed, at some length, the way in which younger potters have gained control in the running of community affairs in Moeran 1984: 150–81.

3

Modern romantic my plan travel

Introduction

One of the interesting points about *sake*-drinking parties in Sarayama concerned the way in which they were used by younger men
to manipulate the elder generation. The relationship between authority and power in language is one that will crop up again when
I examine the role of keywords in the organisation of Japanese
society, but, before that, I want to look at another expression of
potential conflict between generations in contemporary Japanese
society: the language of Japanese tourism.

There must be few people in the Western world for whom the
notion of tourists from Japan is not immediately accompanied
by an image of cameras, flags and sex. Well over four million
Japanese a year have been going abroad since the end of the
1970s. In the mid 1980s, the figure has increased drastically: 5
million in 1986; 6.8 million in 1987; and 8 million in 1988. By
1991, it is anticipated that there will be 10 milion tourists a year
leaving Japan for foreign parts (*The Economist* 1988). Together
with the United States and West Germany, Japan is one of the
three largest international tourist nations in the world. Of those
travelling overseas in the 1980s, a very large percentage are un-
married women and retired couples, while honeymooners occupy
more than half the places available on international package tours
(Nihon Kōtsū Kōsha 1982: 10).

Why do the Japanese travel abroad? What is it that they seek
abroad that they cannot find at home? In the 1960s and 1970s,
their international tourism was geared primarily to sightseeing.
It is mainly middle-aged people who travelled in groups, accompanied by a tour guide. Yesterday the Acropolis, today the Coli-
seum, tomorrow the Eiffel Tower—that was the typical pattern of

a European tour. Nowadays, however, Japanese prefer to travel alone, or in small groups of friends or relatives. They want to experience not sights but action, to 'participate with their own skins' in sports, hobby activities, and such staged events as the Knoxville Expo, the Dutch Floriade or the Aloha Week in Hawaii.[1] It would seem as if it is the younger generation which is altering the face of Japan's international travel and bringing the goals of the country's tourism more in line with those of the West.

The young have only begun to travel abroad in very large numbers since 1975, but their interest in sports in particular would appear to have replaced the former emphasis on group travel and sight-seeing and to have promoted ideas of 'individuality' and 'play'. Tourism is no longer rigidly controlled. The Japanese are being invited to do what they want, as they want, and where they want, and sometimes are required only to reserve their plane seats and hotel accommodation in advance. The era of the flag-bearing uniformed guide leading a party of bewildered Japanese tourists across Trafalgar Square or up the Empire State Building appears to have come to a close.

The language of travel brochures

The idea, particularly prevalent among the young in the mid 1980s, that life is to be enjoyed and that tourism is one of the better ways to enjoy life, has, of course, serious implications for the society and economy of Japan as a whole. Before discussing this, however, I want to consider some of the concepts and phrases with which travel agencies seek to attract people to join their tours. After all, while a number of potential tourists hear about 'thrilling' Waikiki beach, 'exotic' Bangkok, 'glamorous' Monte Carlo, and so on from friends and family, they are, in the end, almost bound to read and be influenced by travel brochures before deciding whether to go to Hawaii, Thailand, or Monaco for their vacations. In other words, the language used in travel brochures is a guide in itself to the aspirations of tourists, and hence to those of Japanese society as a whole—or at least to a major part of it.

So how are these aspirations phrased? The standard Japanese

travel brochure (for a *Look* or *Jalpak* tour, for example) starts out with an introductory page, followed by a list of tour-course varieties and prices. It then devotes one section to hotels, another to food, and a third to the advantages of this particular tour (advantages which tend to emphasise that Japanese-style service still remains with the tourist abroad). The brochure then turns to a description of the sights to be seen and things to be done abroad. As I interpret it, such brochure 'literature' suggests that the Japanese tourist is preoccupied with nature, food and recreation—'Nature' tourism—on the one hand, and with shopping, art, and culture—'Culture' tourism—on the other (Graburn 1977: 27). General themes that recur time and time again are those of status and experience (in the guise of 'discovery', 'authenticity', and 'exoticism').

Nature tourism

One of the major themes of Japanese nature tourism is the appreciation of nature itself. This is hardly unexpected, given the time-honoured Japanese preoccupation with flora and fauna, landscapes, the changing seasons, and so on. A similar appreciation of nature is to be found in the Western (particularly North European) tourist's preoccupation with sun and sea, but the Japanese in fact have not until very recently been concerned with the *physical* advantages to be gained from good weather. Rather, they have regarded nature as something to be spiritually experienced in its totality, and the brochures assure them that it has 'grandeur' (*yūdai*), it is 'beautiful' (*utsukushii*), it is 'artistic' (*geijutsu*), 'magnanimous' (*ōraka*), 'opulent' (*yutaka*), and—perhaps not surprisingly—'unpolluted' (*yogore no nai*). It is depicted in minute detail in descriptions of a hotel garden in Singapore, of the streets of Penang, or of the gentle breezes of the Aegean.

Here three comments need to be made about the Japanese tourists' attitude towards nature. Firstly, their love of nature is, in part at least, stimulated by the fact that economic growth and industrialisation within Japan have led to overcrowded living conditions and to pollution of the environment. This is made clear in the brochures published for domestic tourism, where the contrast between the peace and quiet of Japan's countryside and the noise and bustle of city life is much more obvious.[2]

Secondly, although the Japanese like to experience nature in its totality, it would seem that there is a relatively recent tendency for Japanese tourists to emphasise certain aspects of nature in much the same way as do Western tourists; in other words, they want to make use of nature, and sun and sea are rapidly coming to be associated with and valued for the recreation that they provide. This would appear to be a result of the increase in number of young tourists abroad and of their interest in 'experience' as opposed to mere 'sight-seeing'. The Japanese are in the process of shifting from Graburn's 'environmental' tourism to 'recreational' tourism (1977: 27–8).

Thirdly, the wealth of nature is at times directly contrasted with the naivety or 'artlessness' (*soboku*) of the people living there. This tendency towards 'ethnic' tourism is also to be found in the Japanese predilection for food and shopping (see below).

The first Japanese tourist this author ever met was in Athens, Greece in the summer of 1967. He, and all the others in his party of twenty-five, carried three pieces of hand luggage. Of these—no exaggeration here—two were filled with food! The first Japanese tourists abroad were, for the most part somewhat chary of sampling foreign cooking and took with them, as a precautionary measure, green tea, dried seaweed, pickles, instant noodles and various other Japanese delicacies, in order to survive the rigours of overseas travel. Those days are now mostly (but not entirely) long gone. The Japanese tourist has learned that foreigners can cook after all, and one of the pleasures advertised (and disappointments experienced) in international travel is the food that is consumed. Travel brochures are full of tips on what to eat where: Macao is billed for its Portuguese cooking, Penang for its fresh fish, Vienna for its coffee, Paris for its raw oysters, Geneva for its fondue. Honeymooners are invited to sample 'romantic' dinners with 'tropical' drinks in Singapore, and food—from Alaskan salmon to Hawaiian pineapples—is frequently advertised as one of the better forms of gift to take back home. In short, food is a means by which the Japanese are invited to experience 'being abroad', and the emphasis nowadays on 'variety' (Mexican *tacos*, Spanish *tapas*, Chinese *dim sun*, English roast beef, Indian curries, and so

42

on) shows the extent to which the Japanese are beginning to 'go native'.

Since 1979, Japanese people travelling abroad have begun to want to participate in the activities of the peoples, rather than merely see the sights of the countries, they visit. This trend is expected to continue in the future and would appear to be closely connected with the fact that young people now form a very large percentage of Japanese tourists overseas. It is the latter who are invited to participate in 'active', 'sporty', and 'thrilling' recreational activities. The travel brochures are filled with information on what to do where—surfing, tennis, and riding in Hawaii; fishing, skiing, and golf in Europe; roller skating, cycling and yachting in the United States—and the idea of 'sports' in the Japanese tourist language now includes such activities as jogging and going to discos. In other words, the concept of 'recreation' has been virtually reduced to 'sports'.

Economic factors are partly responsible for young people's preference for 'activity' tourism in the first place, and where they decide to do such activities in the second. As a general rule it can be said that recreation facilities are not readily available to the average Japanese unless he or she is prepared to pay very large membership fees for the use gymnasiums, tennis courts, or golf courses. Young people in particular are not in a position to pay such fees without company or parental financial aid. (For the privilege of being able to participate in American-style keep fit classes, for example, a Japanese may be asked to pay as much as a £1,000 entry fee. Entrance fees for golf clubs run from £3,000 up.) Tourism, therefore, provides them with the opportunity to indulge in the sort of activities that they cannot regularly do at home; at the same time, it allows them to try out locally popular sports that are not widely known or practised in Japan itself. It is probably for these reasons (and the fact that both are within reasonable economic distance of Japan) that Hawaii and the West Coast of America have become such popular targets of Japanese tourism. Skateboarding, surfing, and windsurfing are almost as 'exotic' to the Japanese sportsman as are mangos, mousaka, and macadamia nuts to the Japanese gourmet.

Tourism is basically a product of urbanisation. Up to 1978, almost one in four tourists came from Tokyo (Naikaku Sōridaijin

1979: 73). Those who live in cities are the first to want to get out of what they see as 'artificial' surroundings and go back to 'nature'; it is they who want to eat something other then packaged food and to participate in activities other than those that confine them to milling around inside large blocks of concrete. Hence, the urban city dweller's desire to travel far away and sample 'natural', uncontaminated foods, as well as do something 'natural', and hence healthy, like sports. In this respect, nature tourism becomes, perhaps especially for the Japanese, a 'sacred journey' (Graburn 1977: 17–31).

Culture tourism

'Culture tourism' would appear in some respects to precede 'nature tourism', a fact which is not that surprising when one considers that the very concept of 'culture' is closely tied in with urbanisation once more. This notion of 'culture' is born in cities, and people living in cities make use of it in order to set themselves apart from, and above, those living in the countryside.

Those Japanese who first went abroad as tourists did so as sightseers who wanted not just to experience foreign cultures but to *compare* them with their own. International travel began to be possible for the Japanese just at the time when they were starting to search for their 'roots' and when their interest in national 'traditions' and 'history' was at its height. Thus, the Japanese toured the Acropolis, the White House, and the Louvre, partly to see the monuments themselves and partly to see how they compared with such Japanese monuments as the Tōdaiji temple, the Diet building, and the national art museums.

The theme of shopping, which is emphasized so much in the travel brochures, is very much part of the Japanese tourist's desire to compare life abroad with that back home. This penchant for comparison can lead to 'ethnic' tourism; the traveller purchases Bali's *batik*, Hong Kong silk, and Eskimo arts and crafts as mementos of his or her trip abroad. But in general, the Japanese do not buy such products of ethnic tourism for themselves so much as to be given to others. Shopping abroad, therefore, is emphasised in the brochures because it gives the traveller some indication of the sort of gift s/he can—indeed must—bring home and present to family, friends, and fellow workers. Souvenirs, therefore, do not remind the tourist that s/he has been abroad; they remind those in the tourist's immediate social network that s/he has been abroad (*cf.* Graburn 1983).

Japan is famous for its 'souvenir culture' (*omiyage bunka*) and the giving and receiving of presents form a very important part of everyday social relations and in the Japanese economy as a whole. As of 1981, total expenditure on gifts by the Japanese amounted to $6.5 billion; of this amount $3 billion was spent on seasonal and $2 billion on personal gifts. Regardless of whether the Japanese economy is going through a boom period or temporary recession, the gift industry has a 10–15% increase in turnover every year (Nishio 1982: 5). Politicians in such economically depressed countries as America and the United Kingdom might do well, therefore, to encourage their electorates to indulge in minor forms of potlach. A gift-giving season does wonders for the economy (*cf.* Davis 1972).

At the same time, one of the major preoccupations of the Japanese tourist is that of status. Over the years, the Japanese have been led by persuasive advertising to believe that quality is only to be found in certain 'brand name' commodities. Thus one of the pleasures—and indeed for some, one of the 'musts'—of going abroad is that of being able to purchase a brand name commodity in its country of origin. Japanese tourists make certain that they buy Burberry coats in London, Cardin ties in Paris, or Gucci bags in Rome. It is this kind of shopping item that the Japanese tourist keeps for himself, not just as a reminder of a trip abroad, but as a symbol of status that comes from having been abroad. 'I bought my Philippe-Patek in Mitsukoshi department store' can thus be replaced by the ultra-casual 'Oh! I got that the last time I was passing through Switzerland'.

A second important aspect of Japanese culture tourism is an emphasis on art and culture in the travel brochures. Just as we in the West have learned to expect Florence to be linked with the Renaissance, Egypt with pyramids, and Mexico with the Mayan and Aztec civilisations, Japanese tourist information would appear to be much more specific in its use of 'cultural markers' (MacCannell 1976: 110). Lausanne is heralded as housing the headquarters of the I.O.C. (International Olympic Committee); Geneva's university library houses the room used by Rousseau; the Rhine is noted for the poetry written about it by Heine and Byron, while the Piazza di Spagna becomes the prop for the line: 'It was here that Hepburn walked in the film' (the title of which, *Holiday in Rome,* is in itself too well known amongst the Japanese to need mentioning!). It may be that such specificity is required for a nation that has not developed within the Western cultural tradition (compare the Western traveller to Japan), but there are doubts whether, for example, the average American tourist either knows in the first place, or is later given, the same kind of detailed information when embarking upon a European tour.

This preoccupation with 'culture' is to be seen in the travel brochures' frequent reference to cultural institutions—palaces, universities, cathedrals, ruins, museums, opera houses, and theatres; to historical markers—'baroque', 'gothic', 'medieval', 'Islamic'; and to cultural keywords—history (*rekishi*), tradition (*dentō*), art (*geijutsu*), fine art (*bijutsu*), fashion (*fasshon*), civilization (*bunmei*), and culture itself (*bunka* or *karuchā*). There is also what would seem to me to be an unusual emphasis on art and art institutions: Bali's shadow puppet theatre; Milan's *La Scala* opera theatre; Carmel as an 'artists' town'; New York where the world's artists gather in Soho and Greenwich village; and Paris, of course, hardly needs mentioning for Monmartre and its paraphernalia of 'atelier', 'studios', 'galleries', and art museums—plus a list of cafés likely to be frequented by famous artists. The Japanese are currently going through a phase of 'cultural consciousness' and the travel brochures are mines of foreign cultural information. This might seem paradoxical in view of the new tourist trend toward 'participation', but it should be remembered that a very large percentage of overseas tourists are women and that women are the prime consumers of art and culture.

Status and tourism

Already mentioned is the way in which notions of status affect Japanese tourists' decisions about what to buy where. Considering the relation between social status and international tourism in general, the very idea of 'going abroad' is part and parcel of the Japanese concern for his or her position in society. In this respect, one should perhaps consider who goes abroad and how, where, and when s/he does so.

First of all, what kind of Japanese goes abroad as a tourist? As already intimated, the main travellers are either old or young; those least likely to become tourists are people between their mid-30s and late 50s, mainly because they have families to bring up and cannot afford the luxury of family travel abroad. Tourism is a form of leisure, and the ability to avoid work can be translated into terms of status. The tourist appears to have enough money not to have to bother with such offensive things as work (at least for a time). Hence, when old people travel abroad, it is an indication of their financial status and of their newly found leisure that comes with retirement.

But what of the younger generation of tourists? A large percentage of young people who go abroad are honeymooners. Japanese marriage etiquette now makes it virtually essential that newly wedded couples go abroad for their honeymoons (or at least as far as Okinawa which was officially 'abroad' until it was returned to Japan by the U.S.A. in 1972). Not only this, but a considerable number of honeymooners have a second wedding ceremony in churches in Hawaii or on the West Coast of America. In other words, it is currently fashionable, and hence prestigious, to get married according to Western and Christian, rather than 'traditional' Shinto, beliefs.

Closely connected with marriage is tourism by Japanese girls in their 20s. A large percentage of marriages in Japan are still arranged and a prospective bride's 'character' is still measured by her ability to perform the tea ceremony, arrange flowers, and cook in a Japanese style. To these accomplishments has now been added the status of at least one trip abroad, for the 'modern' housewife is now expected to be able to provide something more than 'traditional' Japanese qualities.

Secondly, one may consider how people go abroad. As related at the beginning of this chapter, the Japanese first went abroad in groups, but now there is a tendency for them to go alone. As with Western tourist nations, the Japanese would appear now to view

47

group travel as being lower in status than individual travel. One reason is economic: package tours are that much cheaper. At the same time, there is currently a strong emphasis on individuality in modern Japanese society and such individuality can also be associated with the notion of elitism.

Status that accrues from the way in which one travels can be seen in the language of tourism. In the travel brochures, facilities at hotels and sports clubs are 'luxurious' and 'gorgeous': everything from shops to stage shows in resort areas are 'high class', 'first class', or 'deluxe'; hotel interiors, meals, and night life are 'extravagant', so that the feeling the tourist gets from experiencing all of these is one of 'richness'. Luxury, and the status that is implied by luxury, is of course to be found in the names of hotels (Royal, Regency, Imperial, etc.); in the class of airline travel (Ambassador, Executive, Clipper, etc.); and in the name of the tour (Special, Royal, Ace, etc).

Thirdly, elitism also derives from the tourist's decision about where to go, for the distance travelled is more or less equivalent to financial status. As a general rule, therefore, it is much 'better' for a Japanese to go to Singapore than it is for him to visit Seoul, and better still to go to America rather than to south-east Asia. 'Destination elitism' would in this respect appear to be culturally relative: What is good for a Japanese tourist is not necessarily so for a traveller from Canada. However, it is possible for a country to be rated high on the Japanese tourist's prestige list despite its proximity to Japan itself. China is a case in point. But it should be noted that the tourist to China would be expected to pay more for his trip there than he would for an equivalent trip to, say, Hawaii. The tourist thus purchases a status which depends not just on distance but on the general development of tourism as a whole in the country he wishes to visit.

Another form of such status is to be found in what may be called 'cultural elitism'. A study of the travel literature suggests that there may be a cultural elitism which is independent of economic status. Japanese travel brochures frequently resort to comparisons of tourist areas in south-east Asia and America with their European counterparts. Thus, Pattaya Beach in Thailand is likened to the south of France; Macao is described as 'the Monte Carlo of the East'; San Francisco is praised for its 'Mediterranean mood' and Boston for its 'European city mood'. This would seem to indicate that for the Japanese. Europe is at the pinnacle of cultural prestige. The fact that Europe is one of the most distant targets of tourism, however, makes it difficult to prove that 'cultural elitism' is independent of 'destination elitism' (*cf.* Gather International 1972–1973).

Perhaps one example of the Japanese admiration for Western culture is to be found in the travel brochures' extravagant use of English and other European language loanwords in their descriptions of sights and amenities abroad. The Japanese tend to use such loanwords in particular when they talk or write about such Western, culturally influenced topics as fashion and pop music, and international tourism is no exception to this rule. Most loanword and phrases in the travel literature consist of descriptive adjectives and nouns. Thus, the Japanese tourist is invited to experience the 'unique', the 'fresh', the 'nostalgic', the 'exotic', the 'thrilling', the 'romantic', the 'sporty', the 'happy', the 'active', the 'moody', the 'modern', and the 'rich', whether in a 'riviera', 'resort', 'surfing mecca', 'shopping arcade', 'downtown area', or wherever. In this respect, the language of international tourism stands in direct contrast with that of domestic tourism, where the emphasis is predominantly on Japanese words—*dokutoku* (the unique), *azayaka* (the fresh), and *natsukashii* (the nostalgic). However, foreign loanwords are used in brochures for domestic travel when the latter are related to city tourism. Literature on a 'Tokyo Graffiti' tour used such words as 'exciting', 'crystal', 'academic', 'romantic', and 'thrilling', thus emphasizing the other side of Japanese tourism, for young people tour to see the lights of the capital. Most domestic tourism, however, focuses on scenic or cultural spots, and for this, typically 'Japanese' phrases are used (cf. Graburn 1983, on Japanese domestic tourism).

Finally, the timing of travel abroad is usually closely connected with status in that there are 'on' and 'off' seasons for tourism; those who can afford the time to holiday during the off-peak season are usually considered in the West to be more 'superior' than if they had gone away with everyone else during the summer vacation period. With Japanese tourism abroad, however, there does not appear to be that much elitism so far as the timing of vacations is concerned. Unlike the French, the Japanese do not of necessity take their vacations in August, for example. This is partly because resorts popular with the Japanese have good weather all year round and partly because the Japanese salaried worker does not take an annual vacation at a fixed time of year. This gives tourists considerable flexibility in the choice of when to take vacations and, hence, disposes of the status myth that derives in other countries from off-peak travel. One suspects, however, that this state of affairs will change with increased family travel and increased holiday periods for the Japanese salaried worker. Tourist peak periods are very closely connected with educational systems. The fact that the Japanese school year begins in April and not in September, for example, has an enormous influence on travel within and outside the country.

Individuality and Japanese society

Tourism is one means by which modern man 'experiences' life. Hence, one of the major themes in the travel brochures is that of 'discovery', as the tourist is invited to experience the thrill of being abroad. 'Discovery! Discovery! At every crossroad', says the blurb on Singapore; 'round one unknown country after another—that is the joy of travel' goes the introduction to a tour of Europe; 'a great experience awaits you: I love New York' (the latter phrase in English) is how the tourist to the East Coast of America is greeted. The tourist literature suggests that the world is waiting to be discovered by you—and you alone. You are the prince who will wake Sleeping Beauty from her timeless dreams with the kiss of your presence!

Yet the tourist is not just an outsider in his or her travels. It is suggested that s/he can be party to the smells, to the laughter, to the fun of an evening in Taipei, Barcelona, or Los Angeles. S/he can 'melt' (*tokekomu*) into his surroundings, 'not just as passing traveller, but in touch with the lives of the local people'. As the Japan Travel Bureau's catchphrase goes: 'Travel is contact' (*tabi wa fureai*). 'Contact' is the vital word.

Now, although this invitation to the tourist to experience 'authenticity' would appear to be common to all tourism (*cf.* Mac-Cannell 1976), it is particularly important so far as the Japanse are concerned because of the way in which their society is organised. In Japan, there has been a strong ideological emphasis on the importance of the group over the individual; and the necessity for the individual to subordinate his or her interests to those of the primary group to which he or she belongs. When Japanese go abroad, they are temporarily without any group affiliation. Escape from the restrictions imposed by the group used to give rise to the popular proverb *tabi no haji wa kakisute:* the tourist could do something 'shameful' precisely because he is traveling on, free of social pressures. Now, however, Japanese are asked to identify with the people they visit and hence avoid that anomalous state of being an 'outsider' (*yoso no mono*).

The idea of 'discovery', therefore, seems to be used to help the Japanese think that they are merging into new surroundings at a time when temporarily cut of from the embrace of family, office, or other primary groups. At the same time, however, the invitation to a Japanese to melt into a foreign society is couched in such language that can only make him—or, more likely, her—more aware of her self in isolation.[3] The world awaits to be discovered by her and her alone. The travel brochures use the direct vocative 'you' (*anata*) in addressing the tourist and there is the pervasive idea that 'you' are always *alone*, that the moods you experience are entirely your own, to be shared perhaps by a loved one, but certainly not by a group of people on the same tour or by the crowds of people thronging the sites or resorts when you get there. This mood is strengthened by photographs of sea, sand, temples, sunsets, and so on with but one or two people depicted in them. The world is yours and nobody else's in tourism. As the brochures say: 'choose your own ...' Shanghai, Brazil, or Polynesia.

This use of the second person to appeal to the individual is not just a trick of the travel trade but one of advertising in general. As we shall see in later chapters, advertisements tend to appeal to the 'individual' in all consumer societies—a characteristic which has, of course, serious implications for the ideology of 'groupness' in contemporary Japan. Tourist literature is thus just one example of a general trend towards making the Japanese extremely self-conscious. Travel brochures use such phrases as 'my pace' or 'my plan' (in English) to make the tourist realise that s/he can do what s/he wants to do once s/he has escaped the confines of Japanese society. The tourist is invited to 'enjoy' herself, to play (*asobu*), to be light-hearted (*kigaru*) when away from an environment in which the importance of work (*shigoto*) and seriousness (*majime*) is stressed. S/he is told to take it easy (*yukkuri*), to be carefree (*nonbiri*), to 'relax', to make use of 'free time', to do as s/he pleases (*kimama*) in a leisurely (*yuttari*), self-composed (*ochitsuita*) and easy (*yutori*) manner. In short, tourists are invited to do all the things that Japanese society has not traditionally permitted them to do—at least, not without the knitted brows and disapproving frown of a Sharaku actor!

Conclusion

The tourist literature is an interesting guide to what would appear to be fundamental changes taking place in Japanese society. It points out contrasts between the tourist's own and other countries' societies. In Japan, the tourist is invited to experience unpolluted nature, nature on a grand scale; s/he is told that s/he can still come across 'artless' peoples of the kind that no longer exist in modern sophisticated societies. International tourism, therefore, appears to threaten the tourist's present social system. It is potentially revolutionary for it invites the tourist to experience change and hence possibly to bring back such change to her own society. Tourism is a bane to the idea that every nation should maintain its own 'cultural identity', and Japan, of course, is a particularly good example of this type of nation. As I have said before, Japanese ideologists—from politicians to academics—have long upheld the idea that Japan is 'unique' and that its culture and traditions will never be fully understood by foreigners.

One major barrier to an outsider's understanding is the Japanese language, which makes use of thousands of Chinese characters and three syllabaries (*hiragana*, *katakana* and the Roman alphabet, *rōmaji*). Japanese linguists like to claim that their language is unrelated to other Asian language groups, hence giving support to the view that the Japanese way of thinking is itself quite 'unique'. But, as I have pointed out above, the language of 'modernity'—of tourism, fashion, popular music, the media, and advertising in general—relies to a very large extent on the use of *gairaigo*, or foreign loanwords, for its appeal. In this respect, the language of Japanese tourism would seem to threaten the 'inscrutability' of Japanese written forms, and to make the language as a whole more accessible to outsiders: barriers can be broken down, thanks to the apparent adoption of Western concepts. In other words, tourist language, as the language of modernity, seems to pose a threat to Japan's 'uniqueness' or sense of 'difference.'

At the same time, adoption may well lead to cultural adaptation, and the frequent use of foreign words in Japanese may serve to shore up the preservation of that which is culturally different and specifically Japanese. The same may be true of the Japanese tourist abroad. If s/he does not find what s/he is looking for in other countries, tourism may end up by reaffirming the superiority of Japan's cultural identity. Potentially revolutionary, the ideals and language of tourism could end up by being 'reactionary'—a point to which I shall return when I discuss Californian car-lore.

The wording of travel brochures, however, shows that the concerns of the Japanese tourist *are* in fact mainly those of the European and American tourist. This would suggest that industrialisation, urbanisation, and consumerism give rise to a similar type of 'modern' person and that cultural differences between nations are disappearing in much the same way as they have done locally within more advanced nations.

One of the major indications of the merging of cultural identities between Japan and other industrialised nations would seem to be the emphasis on individuality (*kosei*), mentioned earlier. The travel brochures' stress on the concepts of play (*asobi*) and contact (*fureai*) would seem to be invitations to the Japanese to disregard the hitherto propagated group ideology. The man who 'plays' is being asked to withdraw from all the moral and social restrictions connected with work. The woman who is told to value 'heart contact' (*kokoro no fureai*) is being told to meet people and situations on her own, independent of group affiliations. *Asobi, fureai* and *kosei* are three words vital not just to tourism but to advertising in general. A department store will display the slogan, 'You're not alive until you learn to play' (*Asobi o sen to ya umarekemu*, Matsuya). An insurance company makes claim to your money by stressing that it 'values heart contact' (*Kokoro no fureai o daiji ni suru*, Nissan Seimei). And a fashion catchphrase links women's clothing with 'love and individuality' (*Ai to kosei no fasshon*, Nagai).

If the language of tourism *is* the same as the language of other aspects of consumerism in industrial societies—from the consumption of alcoholic drinks to that of art—then it is clear that a study of such language can provide us with a clue to the 'structure of modernity' in Japan. According to MacCannell (1976: 2), the fragmented aspect of modernity is a mask. Two points need to be made about this idea. Firstly, the study of tourism *per se* shares this fragmented aspect in anthropology's approach to the study of modern society. Yes, the experience of tourism is the experience of society, but an experience of society that appears to have been created by the media (McLuhan 1964). Secondly, modernity is clearly *not* fragmented, so far as the *language* of tourism, advertising, aesthetics and other aspects of popular culture in contemporary Japan are concerned. Rather, as we shall see in the following chapter, the linguistic mask is used to conceal the fragmentary nature of Japanese society and display its apparent unity.

Notes

1 A greatly publicised aspect of 'skin participation' is to be found in the all-male sex tours around the capitals of south-east Asia.
2 Some interesting aspects of domestic tourism are discussed by Martinez 1989.
3 I say 'her' not simply because the majority of tourists are woman, but because women are obliged by the nature of Japanese society to experience extreme isolation when they leave their natal family for that of their husbands.

4

Keywords and the Japanese 'spirit'

Introduction

I have suggested that there is in Japan what may be called a 'structure of modernity' and that this structure is revealed by the language of consumerism. By focusing on tourism, I showed that there was a conflict between the ideals by which Japanese society is organised (group loyalties, diligence, seriousness) and those expressed in tourist brochures (individuality, leisure, play). Given that the majority of those participating in the kind of 'modern romantic my plan travel' described are young people—especially young women—tourism would seem to point to a division between older and younger generations, on the one hand, and between men and women, on the other.

Throughout the previous chapter, however, I was careful not to make this division too clear cut. International tourism, I said, *may* threaten contemporary Japan's social system; the travel brochures' stress on such concepts as 'play', 'contact' and 'individuality' *seemed* to be an invitation to younger Japanese to disregard group ideals. The reason for my using such imprecise language was not merely to satisfy an academic's propensity for woolly thought. I am not in fact convinced that tourism *does* point to inter-generational or gender divisions. Nor that words like *kosei*, which I have loosely translated as 'individuality', really *do* mean what they appear to mean. It is the fuzzy meanings of words that I want to take up in this chapter on high school baseball, pottery aesthetics and advertising language.

Keywords and the Japanese 'spirit'

In his book *The Cultural Definition of Political Response* the anthropologist David Parkin looks at culture as a system of communications and responses. Custom, he says, consists of conventionalised activity, concept and lexicon, and he suggests that none of these need necessarily reflect the others consistently. Each is thus to some degree autonomous and it is *words* which Parkin argues are the most likely part of custom to persist, even though the content of what they describe may change. These words he refers to as 'key verbal concepts' which 'shape people's perceptions of changes in the group's environment of opportunity, which may in turn redefine the lexicons and taxonomies' (Parkin 1978: 26). In other words, although I suggested right at the beginning of this book that Japanese attitudes towards the relation between their language and culture smack somewhat of the stronger version of the Whorfian hypothesis (that a people's world view is strongly influenced—if not determined—by the grammar of the language it speaks), perceptions are also importantly affected by *lexical* categories.

How useful is Parkin's approach to my own discussion? During my years of research into the production, marketing and aesthetic appraisal of pottery in Japan, I have discovered that a considerable part of the aesthetic vocabulary used by potters, critics and general public is to be found in other spheres of Japanese culture—sports, advertising, tourism, even (as we shall discover later) personalised licence plates on Californian cars. It is clear that there are a number of 'key verbal concepts', or keywords, which occur right across the board in Japanese society and that these can largely be grouped for convenience under the heading of '*seishin*', or 'spirit', a concept which although officially looked down upon after the Pacific War because of its former association with nationalism and militarism, now appears to be regaining some of its former status among the Japanese.

In this chapter, I want to examine the notions that are seen to make up the concept of *seishin*, and to this end I have brought in observations on high school baseball, art pottery and advertising language. My aim is to point out the way in which Japanese society is trying to grapple with the problem of individualism which is commonly feared to accompany Westernisation, modernisation, urbanisation and industrialisation. It is the ambivalence of certain keywords within the concept of *seishin* that allows individualism to challenge the notion of 'selflessness' inherent in the *seishin* model. Yet this same ambivalence has so far prevented Japanese society from jumping—lemming-like—into the abyss of Western individualism, and allows it to retain strong community values.

Models of Japanese social organisation

At the very beginning of this book, I mentioned that there has been some discussion among anthropologists studying Japan concerning the role of the individual in relation to that of the group in Japanese social organisation. This has led to a number of eminent forbears being attacked for expounding a 'group' model which fails to take account, it is said, of a number of facts in Japanese society which contradict this model. The time has come now to take this argument a little further.

First, what is meant by the term 'group model'? In fact, its content is easily grasped, if only because for some time now it has been used by the Japanese themselves to project an image of their country here in the West. We have learned to accept this model and even in some cases—in particular where economics and art are concerned—to imitate its tenets. Briefly put, the group model of Japanese society assumes that people prefer to act within the framework of a group and that such a group will be hierarchically organised and run by a paternalistic leader. The psychological process underlying this structure is called '*amae*', or 'passive love'. Doi (1981: 38) argues that the parent/child relationship naturally creates *amae* and that this feeling comes under the rubric of '*ninjō*', or 'spontaneously arising feeling'. When this parent/child relation of indulgence and dependence is introduced into other relationships, we have what is known as *giri*, or 'socially contracted dependence'. It is the combination of *giri* and *ninjō* which permeates all social relationships, in particular those between leader and subordinate in a group.

According to this model, members of a group are expected to conform and co-operate with one another, to avoid open conflict and competition. The emphasis, therefore, is on harmony, and behaviour tends to be ritualised and formal in order to reduce or eliminate conflict or embarrassment (as we saw in the chapter on *sake* drinking). Ideally, in this king of group, people are supposed to subordinate individual interests to group goals and to remain loyal to group causes. In return for their loyalty and devotion, the leader of the group treats his followers with benevolence and magnanimity (Befu 1980: 170–1).

The trouble with the group model as outlined here is that it fails to encompass certain paradoxes. For example, despite the emphasis on hierarchical forms of organisation in Japanese society, egalitarian forms do exist. Moreover, paternalistic leaders do not necessarily look after the welfare of their subordinates. This can be seen in the organisation of smaller businesses in particular, where employees for their part are not so loyal to their employers. In other words, the group model fails to account for behaviour that goes against group norms. Finally, the ideology of harmony does not explain the conflict and competition rife—as we have seen—in some areas of Japanese society (see also Smith 1978).

Befu rightly argues that the group model does not account for these differences between ideology and behaviour, and that it fails to explain how groups as such are related to one another externally, since it concentrates on their internal structure. He suggests, therefore, that we accept the 'group' model as 'behavioural ideology' and then considers the notion of social exchange, together with the concept of '*seishin*', as an alternative means of explaining the paradoxes outlined above. This social exchange model is far more practical and less overtly ideological than the group model. It assumes that the individual has certain resources such as wealth, knowledge, skills or influential friends, which s/he can exchange with others for resources that s/he does not possess. Here the individual will tend to 'maximize his opportunities by strategically allocating his resources, distributing them to individuals who need them most and are most likely to bring him bountiful returns' (Befu 1980: 179). This does not mean that group ideology and social exchange are mutually exclusive. A company can advocate 'benevolence', but be benevolent only in so far as it is profitable for the company to be so; workers can advocate 'loyalty' to the company, but leave the company if greater loyalties take precedence. Thus the group model is motivated by altruism, the social exchange model by self-interest (*ibid.* p. 180).

Befu's suggestion that we consider social exchange when analysing Japanese society is sensible. It allows us to take account of the role of personal networks (*tsukiai*) which have been almost totally ignored by anthropologists espousing the 'group model'. Yet one frequently finds that people make use of *tsukiai* to break down the altruistic morality of their own group and to threaten the solidarity of an outside group. The group model of Japanese society is unable to explain this.

Finally, Befu suggests that *seishin* is an analytical concept which can be used objectively to explain Japanese social organisation. He takes the concept to refer to individuals *qua* individuals without reference to their social obligations. I would argue, however, that in fact *seishin* is part of that which Befu observes and that, as a result, the concept cannot be applied in this way. He unreflexively uses a Japanese cultural principle to explain Japanese society, and so himself becomes victim of the Japanese group ideological model of which *seishin* is a part. Befu ends up talking about the way people say things ought to be done, and not about the way things actually are done.

So what is *seishin*? In that it is a key verbal concept and hence ambivalent, it is virtually impossible to say precisely what constitutes Japanese 'spirit'. 'Essentially', *seishin* refers to one's inner being which often derives spiritual fortitude from self-discipline. Both Confucian and Buddhist ideals are found in *seishin*, which relies on physical training as a means towards attaining spiritual well-being and harmony within the self. *Bushidō*, the way of the *samurai*, and other martial arts such as *kendō*, *jūdō* and *karate*, together with a number of more 'refined pursuits' such as the tea ceremony, flower arrangement, *sumi* ink painting and calligraphy, all contain strong elements of *seishin* in their instruction and practice. It is only by cultivating *seishin* that one can begin to grasp the 'real essence' of these activities.

The high school baseball tournament

Probably one of the best ways of examining *seishin* in action is by looking at the high school baseball tournament, played annually at the beginning of August at Kōshien Stadium, Osaka. From early in July, high schools all over the country compete in knock-out competitions played at the prefectural level. These are written up in some detail in the newspapers, in particular by the *Asahi* which acts as official sponsor of the annual tournament. The winners of each prefectural competition are then eligible to play at Kōshien, the shrine-like Mecca to the game of baseball in Japan. Each team makes the pilgrimage to Osaka and the cameras of the press are ready to record for posterity the looks and actions of these teenage players as they find themselves stepping on to the turf of the vast arena. It is here that the nation's summer ritual takes place.[1] For ten days, approximately fifty teams battle in gladiatorial combat to receive the accolade of being Japan's 'Number 1' high school team. During these ten days, more than 400,000 people come to watch the games being played at Kōshien. In addition a very large percentage of the population watches the games that are played in temperatures frequently exceeding 35 degrees Centigrade.

As the competition proceeds towards its climax, tension mounts all over the country. Teams are discussed, pitchers and batters assessed, and favourites for the coveted title picked out. As in all knock-out competitions of this nature, there is always the excitement of an upset victory, of some distant country team scrambling through to the quarter finals to challenge the giants—the schools like PL Gakuin, Waseda Jitsugyō, or Chūkyō in Aichi Prefecture—which tend to get through to the last stages of the competition year after year. For the winners of each round there is always the next match to be played; for the losers there are only tears, tears which mingle with the sweat and dust on the players' cheeks at the end of the day. And at the end of the tournament comes *o-bon*, the mid-summer All Souls weekend when the ancestors are believed to return home from the land of darkness. And after All Souls the summer is generally deemed to have 'finished', in that the hot and sticky weather can only get cooler. The high school baseball tournament thus heralds All Souls *o-bon* and *o-bon* heralds the end of the summer.

Every team brings with it its cheer-leaders and supporters. These are marshalled in the enormous Alps Stand, filling the first or third base side of the home plate, depending on which of the two dug-outs their team is occupying. Supporters bring with them their own brass bands (which one after the other proceed to play exactly the same music, every game all day, every day all the tournament). They have uniform-clad boys with arm bands and head bands inscribed with the almost magical words 'hisshō' ('certain victory'). In their white-gloved hands they hold open fans which they swish dramatically through the lifeless, heavy air in order to get their supporters shouting for their team. Down the aisles between seats, girls in bright yellow or pink frilly short dresses wave pom-poms in unison, and the supporters themselves may well be wearing headbands inscribed 'hisshō' and shouting the repetitive chant of 'Wasshoi! Wasshoi!', as they rhythmically beat out their band's tune with wooden spoons for serving rice. The whole scene is reminiscent of American college football with its climax at the Rose Bowl, and the tournament has been compared in significance with the Stanley Cup play-offs in ice hockey and the World Cup finals in soccer (Whiting 1977: 2). N.H.K., the Japanese National Broadcasting Company, televises every game in the tournament, from nine in the morning to six in the evening, and as the days go by, it sometimes seems as though there is hardly a radio or television set in the country which is not tuned in to the live converage. Japanese themselves admit that kōkō yakyū, as high school baseball is called, is one of Japan's last remaining festivals. In that television has made this 'festival' available to the whole nation, one could argue, I think, that high school baseball is one of the very first truly national festivals, participated in by a vast majority of the Japanese people, from taxi drivers in Tokyo to fishermen in Hokkaido and potters in Kyushu.

Now, if the annual high school baseball tournament is, as I have here suggested, a modern Japanese ritual, we need to consider the way in which radio and television commentators present the rites. For it is they who act as 'high priests' for the nation, they who decide what to emphasise or ignore as they intone the 'prayers' surrounding each game. The language that they use is the language through which the nation unites. They may decide to characterise two opposing teams as 'guile' versus 'strength' (waza tai chikara), and use this as a theme around which to build their commentaries. Alternatively, they may decide to call one team by a nickname such as the 'sawayaka eleven' and so stress the 'fresh' attitude to the game taken by an out-of-town team which can only muster eleven players in all. Each team, then, tends so be given some kind of characteristic, some point by which it may be recognised in future matches if it survives the present contest. The easiest way for commentators to do this is to concentrate on the pitcher, or 'ace' as he tends to be termed. It is the pitcher's performance which is generally discussed 90 per cent of the time any team is in the field, and the whole of each game revolves around the pitcher's ability to master opposing batters. The cameramen follow the announcers' cue and zoom in on the pitcher's face. We see every twitch of his mouth, every bead of perspiration that breaks out on his neck and brow. We are forced into sharing his agony when things go wrong, into shedding tears of joy with him when he finally wins a game. The pitcher is the 'hero' when his team wins; he is the sacrificial victim if his team loses. He is interviewed at the end of every game by a bevvy of reporters who ask reactions to certain stages in the progress of the contest.[2] His answers are short, his demeanour humble for a 'hero', for he has to conform to social expectations. Just as Nelson expected every man to do his duty at Trafalgar, so do the Japanese as a whole expect every pitcher and every high school baseball player to do his duty during the tournament. Above everything else, regardless of whether one wins or loses, the rite must be performed in the correct manner.

Ultimately, what is deemed to be responsible for a 'correct manner' is *seishin*, or 'spirit'. It is a player's 'spiritual' attitude and strength which makes or breaks him when it 'comes to the crunch' (*ōzume o mukaeru*). It is here that the commentators really come into their own, for they can draw upon a large vocabulary of keywords to describe the spiritual battle which every pitcher is expected to fight and win if the team as a whole is to survive until the next round. They will use a word such as '*shōbu*', that inimitable oxymoron of 'win' and 'lose' meaning 'competition' or 'contest'. The pitcher throws a '*shōbu*' ball which, if all goes well, will find an 'austere' (*kibishii*) corner of the strike zone. But if a runner reaches first or second base, the mood switches to one of anxiety. The pitcher is facing a 'pinch', a tight spot that can develop into a Sisyphean-like 'mountain' (*ōki na yama*) if things get worse. Then he is expected to 'endure' (*gaman*) the situation, to 'compete to the bitter end' (*ganbaru*) and be 'staunch' (*shikkari shite moraitai*). And if the pitcher somehow succeeds in overcoming the odds against him, in getting a double play for example, he is then praised for 'sticking to it' (*nebari*) and for showing his 'fortitude' (*shinbōzuyoi*). As things get better, the way he 'sticks his chest out' (*mune o haru*), and throws with 'resolve' (*omoikitte*). He 'gives everything' (*isshôkenmei ni*) to the game and wins thereby the final accolade.

This is the way in which almost every game is portrayed in high school baseball. (It is also, of course, the way in which many English public schools like to teach their aspiring gentlemen pupils the art of such team sports as rugger, hockey and rowing.) The teams which reach the final of the tournament are those which have shown real spirit, which have shown 'no wish to escape' (*nigeru kimochi nai*) mental hardship. Finally, it is all over. In the Lévi-Straussian way (1966: 32), from two teams that started as equals, one has emerged the winner. And yet the 'disjunction' of the game is at very same time 'conjoined' by the ritual of the tournament as a whole and by *seishin* in particular. The pitcher of the winning team is embraced; the players run to the home plate to line up and doff their caps to the opposing team and umpires. The winners then line up for the last time to hear their school song played over the tannoy system and to watch their school flag being run up the masthead above the scoreboard. Cameras zoom in once more on the tear-stained faces of the victors, and on the crouched bodies of the losers who kneel dejected in the dust and scoop up handfuls of sacred Kōshien stadium earth to put in their kitbags and take as souvenirs back home. The commentators praise the losers, and then the song of victory is played.[3] We come to the Closing Ceremony, with its speeches pointing out that the winners 'have given their all to the last moment' (*saigo made zenryoku o tsukushite*) and 'adorned history' (*rekishi o kazaru*) with the 'marvellous quality' (*rippa na naiyō*) of their game. Now there is only 'next year' to look forward to, with this year's competition 'full of memories' and 'impressions' that will remain imprinted on our minds. Gold medals with crimson ribbons are placed around he necks of the winners; silver medals with purple ribbons around those of the runners-up. Then both teams march to the scoreboard to partici-pate in the final flag-lowering ceremony. The 'tournament song' is played, and then the national anthem as the *hinomaru* Japanese national flag is lowered. The ritual is finally over. Goodbye heroes! You have played your part and given back the Japanese people their 'spirit' for another year.

Seishin and the group model

In his *City life in Japan,* Dore (1958: 67) comments that: 'the old Japanese belief that *seishin*—spirit, will-power—could conquer matter, that the human body would endure loss of sleep, starvation and physical pain to an almost unlimited degree provided the will was strong enough, has demanded some modification ever since the central wartime inference from this premise—that Japanese spirit would be superior to American guns and bombs—has been falsified'. While he suggested that the ideology of *seishin* was not nearly as important as it used to be, Frager and Rohlen, writing almost twenty years later, have argued to the contrary, and show how *seishin* acts as a kind of interpretative lens through which the Japanese like to view their own culture and society. After showing how broadly the concept is used throughout Japanese society—by companies, government agencies, schools of art and religious bodies—Frager and Rohlen stress its ideological importance to the notion that Japanese society is 'unique' and 'group oriented'. One passage is, I think, worth quoting to see the resemblance between the concept of *seishin* and the group model criticised by Befu.

> The seishin outlook does not see the world as inherently divided into class or other interest groups; it chooses to view individuals less in terms of age, wealth, and the like, and more in terms of 'spiritual' strength or weakness; it urges a sense of gratitude to others and to society rather than criticism or cynical detachment; it de-emphasizes the possibilities for doctrinal discussion or dispute in favour of psychological change and awakened personal experience; it considers order, individual sacrifice, dedication, hierarchy, thorough organization, a disregard for material disadvantages, and group activity to be expressions of proper attitudes and spirit, and it views traditional teachings and practices as consis ent with modern science and industrial society, in effect saying that there is much more that is of timeless value in the tradition (Frager & Rohlen 1976: 270).

Here we find a number of concepts that I have already mentioned in my description of the high school baseball tournament:

'strength', 'fortitude' and 'perseverance' (*nebari, shinbō, gaman, nintai, kurō, ganbaru,* etc.); 'single-mindedness' (*omoikitte, seijitsu, makoto*) and 'group spirit' (*dantai ishiki, minna to issho*). At the same time, the concept of *seishin* also includes ideas of 'self discipline' (*enryo*), 'loyalty' and 'devotion' (*giri, on, chū, kō*), which have been used by scholars such as Benedict (1946) and Doi (1981) to explain the workings of Japanese society. Indeed, I remember very well one evening towards the end of my four-year stay in Kyushu when I was called away to attend a meeting of parents at the local primary school. There was a 'discussion' during which the problems of modern youth were talked about (in the kind of rambling, monologue-type speeches that the Japanese adopt to discuss things): why were the young taking to violence? Why didn't they do as they were told any more? Why was the family not as strong a social unit as it used to be? The answers that were provided by the school headmaster were all to do with *seishin,* and included mention of Mencius, Confucius, as well as of 'discipline' (*kiritsu*), 'order' (*chitsujo*), 'meekness' (*sunao*), 'responsibility' (*sekinin*), 'goodwill' (*kōi*), and so on and so forth. The situation illustrated precisely the paradox pointed out by Frager and Rohlen: that the concept of *seishin* is likely to thrive in a Japanese society undergoing change. As Austin (1976: 8) puts it in his introduction to their article: 'the more rapid the change, the more traumatic its effects and the more in demand the qualities of endurance, strength and perseverance that provide a stable set of values to grasp as an empirical aid in coping with a society that fosters insecurity'. *Seishin* is being called upon to combat what are seen to be the evils of Western capitalism and individualism. Somehow people—especially young people—have to be guided into identifying with a 'Japaneseness' which will conquer these evils.

Aesthetics and advertising

If this supposition is correct, we should expect to find the concept of *seishin* being used not only in baseball (or other sports), but right across society. I have already shown how in fact anthropologists dealing with Japan have tended to rely on aspects of *seishin* in their interpretations of the structure of Japanese society. Now I consider keywords used in the criticism of art pottery and in newspaper, magazine and television advertising to see whether we cannot in fact isolate certain other concepts which are part and parcel of the Japanese 'spirit'. It is here that I will turn my attention to Japan's 'internal cultural debate'.

Japanese art pottery is a fairly recent phenomenon which first came to public attention during the Taishō period (1912–1926). Although pottery came to be included in the Imperial Art Exhibition (*teiten*) in 1927, it was not until the 1950's, with the establishment by the government of a system of Important Intangible Cultural Properties, that potters were able to get their work accepted as 'art' by Japanese society in general (Moeran 1987).

With the birth of pottery as an art form, critics have come to play an important role in publicising the way in which pottery ought to be made and appreciated. In describing modern art pottery, critics tend to use words such as 'staunch' (*shikkari shita*) or 'stable' (*antei shita*) to describe form. These are words both frequently used of baseball pitchers, volleyball teams, professional golfers and so on. The potter is admired for his 'brave' (*yūki*) and 'conscientious' (*teinei*) work in just the same way as sportsmen are admired. If a potter is to be criticised, then he will be criticised in much the same manner as is the high school baseball pitcher. Words like 'soft' (*amai*) 'weak' (*yowai*) and 'dull' (*nibui*) will be used by both critic and commentator alike, who are convinced that both artist and sportsman must 'suffer' (*kurō/kurushimu*) to achieve success. The life of the artist is as 'austere' (*kibishii*) as that of the sportsman, and such austerity should be readily perceptible in his work.

All these words would appear to fit the *seishin* model outlined earlier. Yet another factor which is seen to make a pitcher's hurling or potter's throwing at the wheel good is the concept of 'life'. A ball 'without life' (*ikite'nai*) will be hit into the stands; a pot 'without life' will never become accepted as 'art'. So commentators and critics alike look for the ball or pot that is alive (*tama/katachi ga ikiteiru*). Although it is clearly difficult, if not impossible, to decide by objective criteria what constitutes 'life' in either of these contexts, it would appear that such a characteristic can come only from a sportsman's or potter's 'heart' (*kokoro*).

The concept of 'heart', like all important keywords, is not just polysemic. Speakers also very widely in their views on the appropriateness of its use in a given context. Some might prefer to translate the term by the word 'mind' rather than 'heart', but for reasons which will, I think, become clear I shall retain the word 'heart'. At times, *kokoro* is used as part of the 'disciplined' spirit discussed at such length here. In the closing speech of the high school baseball tournament, for example, one of the officials praised the players' 'assiduous hearts' (*kokoro no tannen*). At other times, however, *kokoro* would appear to be opposed to *seishin*. In the appreciation of pottery, for example, I have heard the concept of 'heart' being used in direct antithesis to 'skill' (*gijutsu bakkashi, kokoro nashi*, 'all skill and no heart'), and since a potter's mastery of technical skill is generally thought to depend on his *seishin*, 'heart' and 'spirit' here find themselves in opposition. Yet, at the same time, 'skill' is a word used with some pride by manufacturers of consumer goods (*cf*. 'the skill of Citizen' (*gijutsu no Citizen*); 'the advanced skills of Nissan, loved by all the world' (*sekai ni aisareru, senshin gijutsu no Nissan*)). This suggests that, in other circumstances, *kokoro* could stand for 'Japaneseness' *vis-à-vis* Western technology. Thus it seems to me that *kokoro* in Japanese currently occupies a somewhat ambivalent position in the country's internal cultural debate, and that it is being used to play a double role, half in, half out of, *seishin*. This can be seen in the way critics expect potters to 'put their heart' into their work (*kokoro no komotta shigoto*), while at the same time demanding that their heart be filled with 'pleasure' (*kokoro no tanoshisa*) and 'play' (*kokoro no asobi*). But notions of 'pleasure' and 'play' are normally alien to the concept of spirit (*seishin*).

The point to note here is that art pottery is not simply a product made by man; it is a consumer item, transformed by the qualities perceived to exist in it by people who appreciate pottery. As in much English or European art criticism, the qualities of the artist are seen by the Japanese to pervade the pottery that he or she produces. In this way the art object serves to link consumer to producer, and it is the heart or *kokoro* which does this. Whatever else it may be unable to do, a pot must 'strike the heart' (*kokoro ni uttaeru*) of the person who sees it.

It is not surprising to find, therefore, that the much discussed aesthetic concepts of *sabi*, translated by Kenkyusha's dictionary as 'elegant simplicity', and *wabi*, or 'quiet taste', are seen by one critic to mean 'the involvement of one person with another' (*hito to hito to no kakariai*). This attitude is frequently found in advertising, where 'contact between hearts' (*kokoro no fureai*) is a popular catchphrase in Japanese copy writing. Indeed, the word *kokoro* was the most commonly used word in advertising in Japan during the 1970s.[4] Other words common to both aesthetic criticism and to advertising are 'generous' (*ōraka*), 'tranquil' (*odayaka*), 'fresh' (*azayaka*), 'invigorating' (*sawayaka*), 'abundant' (*yutaka*), 'intimate' (*hitashii*), and so on. All these words connote properties attributable to the 'heart' and are spontaneous aspects of an individual's purposeful action, rather than of what I regard as the socially imposed discipline of *seishin*. Words used as expressions of the 'heart' are not nearly as socially constraining as those like *gaman*, *shinbō*, *nebari* and so on which form the Japanese 'spirit'. They include, moreover, a number of English loanwords such as 'sharp', 'clear', 'vitality', 'rhythm', 'dynamic', 'originality', 'simple' —all of these frequently taking the place of Japanese words of fairly equivalent meaning. When Japanese talk about the 'heart', they talk also of 'human life' (*jinsei*). Pottery should be imbued with 'the charm of human life' (*jinsei no uruoi*); Heineken beer with 'the taste of human life' (*jinsei, ajiwatte ikitai*). And closely connected with 'human life' is the newly fashionable word 'individual' or 'idiosyncratic' (*kosei*). Art pottery has to be 'individually creative' (*koseiteki na sakuhin*) to be beautiful; Gauloises cigarettes are advertised as 'individual to the very end' (*doko made mo koseiteki*); a Daihatsu car as 'individual is beautiful' (*koseiteki'tte utsukushii*); and Fuji xerox copiers as 'fresh ... precise ... and individual' (*azayaka de are ... seikaku de are ... koseiteki de are ...*). *Kosei* is rapidly joining *kokoro* as the 'in word' of the 1980s.

This brings me to the related problems of group and individual, Japan and the West. In a survey which I conducted recently, visitors to art museums in Japan were asked to distinguish between the concepts of 'traditional beauty' (*dentōbi*) and 'modern beauty' (*gendaibi*) in Japanese art pottery. One word that was typically used to describe 'modern' beauty was 'individuality' (*kosei*); another that I found to be typical of 'traditional' beauty was 'no mind' or 'no heart' (*mushin*). These two words were almost invariably used mutually exclusively. In other words, people felt that it was only by being without mind, by being 'detached' if you like, that 'traditional' beauty could be born (in the days before Westernisation), but that nowadays a potter had to put some of his 'individuality' into his work in order to create 'modern' beauty (and the passive/active distinction of 'being born' and 'creating' was also made). Here we have an opposition not simply between 'individuality' and 'no mind', but also between 'heart' (*kokoro*) and 'no mind' (*mushin*, which is written with the character for 'heart' with a negative prefix). *Mushin* is very much part of the *seishin* ideal in which the self is subordinated in the interests of harmony; *kokoro* is also part of the *seishin* ideal, and yet *kokoro* cannot logically exist side by side with *mushin*, for it expresses the presence of heart or mind.

Clearly, *kokoro* is a pivotal keyword in Japan's internal cultural debate because it allows non-Japanese ideas to be included in people's perceptions of society. I have already mentioned how English loan words (which include concepts such as 'originality' generally alien to Japanese aesthetics) are brought in under the umbrella of *kokoro*. Here we see *kokoro* moving right out of the *seishin* model to incorporate essentially Western concepts. Similarly, we find advertising messages such as 'Bring about the revolution of the heart!' (*kokoro no kakumei o okosu*), and 'You have heart, you have abundance' (*kokoro ga aru, yutakasa ga aru*), where 'abundance' ultimately refers to the affluence that accompanies capitalism.

And yet *kokoro* does not necessarily have to support Western ideals that go against the concept of *seishin*. A large number of advertisements tend to emphasise the personal relations that Japanese value so greatly. 'Dial a phone number and dial a heart' (*denwa o kakeru ... kokoro o kakeru*), 'Your heart is delivered, your heart smells so fragrant' (*kokoro ga todokimasu, kokoro ga kaorimasu*), and other such catchphrases stress the importance of relationships between people in Japanese society. Thus, however individualistic you are invited to be, you are often invited to be individualistic *for somebody*. Hence a catchphrase such as 'Your heart, your beauty' (*anata no kokoro, anata no utsukushisa*) is an invitation for you to become beautiful both for yourself and on behalf of others. In the background, the concept of *seishin* looms again, for—as in art—you are being advised that ultimately beauty derives from an inner spiritual discipline.

Here then, I see a second role for *kokoro*. As I said earlier, *seishin* tends to dictate the way in which people *ought* to behave in Japanese society; it prescribes formal relations of *giri*, duty, and *on*, indebtedness. *Kokoro*, even within the *seishin* model, allows for variations and stresses the alternative to *giri*, the concept of *ninjō* or 'spontaneity'. We have seen that *giri* is socially contracted interdependence and *ninjō* a spontaneous feeling. Emphasis on the former, I suggest, gives rise to the group model explanation of Japanese society; emphasis on the latter to that of social exchange. However, as Befu admits, neither can exist without the other. The ever-present danger is that *ninjō* can become ego-centred action. Thus, by using the word *kokoro*, the Japanese aim at solving, first, the inherent problem of the relationship between *giri* and *ninjō*, and secondly, the external problem of group vis-à-vis individual, of Japan against the West.

And yet, because of the flexibility of *kokoro*, which has now come to be used as a keyword in Western-style capitalist consumerism, *kokoro* is also found in a dialogue with *kosei*, or the individual. This dialogue would seem directly to contradict the 'selfless detachment' of *mushin* and to tread a semantic tightrope strung between the two points of spontaneity and social exchange, on the one side, and outright individualism and 'negative reciprocity', on the other (see Figure 4).

But I say 'would seem to contradict' with reason. Ultimately, I am not convinced that *kosei* actually is equivalent to what we know as 'individualism' in the West. The Japanese are extremely suspicious of such 'individualism', and the interesting point is that the word for 'individualism' (*kojinshugi*), is in fact viewed entirely *negatively*.[5] In other words, the Japanese see only the worst aspects of Western-style individualism in *kojinshugi* ('negative reciprocity' in the diagram). The good side of our 'individualism' is not to be found in the concept of *kojinshugi*, but in that of *kosei*. This means that the Japanese are in effect denying that there is any good at all in Western individualism and that *kosei* is in fact entirely original and hence 'uniquely Japanese'. In this way, the

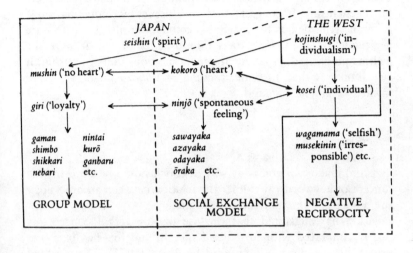

Figure 4: Interpretation of Japanese social organisation through keywords

advantages of Western individualism are being neatly adopted and adapted into *seishin*, or 'Japanese spirit'. To adopt the parlance of Le Carré's spy circus, *kokoro* is thus a double agent, while *kosei* is the 'mole' in the internal cultural debate, in which the West was defeated long ago without ever realising it.

So we are back to square one. That *kokoro* is the most popular word in Japanese advertising copy represents at one level the triumph of irrational 'feeling' over rational 'mind'; it suggests that all debate on the issues of capitalism, of which advertising is the mouthpiece, is stifled (*cf.* Williamson 1978: 13). At another level, *kokoro's* use poses a more fundamental question concerning the relation between the Japanese and Western concept of 'mind'. Western culture and Western technology are seen by the Japanese as products of Cartesian rationalism. They have revered Western culture and technology over the past century, only to discover that both leave much to be desired. There is something 'missing'; the Western mind is too limited in its horizons and the Japanese mind feels that it has grasped all that can be offered by the West and has room to spare. This is where *kokoro* comes in. It is essentially a Japanese concept which, it is claimed, understands beyond mere 'intellectualism'. It suggests that such issues as individualism—generally regarded as the inevitable companion of capitalism—are irrelevant to Japan. *Kokoro* is thus used as though it were the melting point of all Japanese in one harmonious unity of *seishin*. It also intimates that an understanding of *kokoro* might also lead towards a united mankind.

Conclusion

I wish to make two points by way of conclusion: one concerns the concept of keywords; the other the relation between anthropology and a society's internal cultural debate.

Parkin has suggested that the use of key verbal concepts is closely connected with formalised speech, and this has been the gist of the argument put forward by Bloch (1975). The work of both these writers has centred on the political usage of keywords and on how they may stifle the exchange and expression of new ideas and so maintain the *status quo*, with Parkin stressing how their ambivalence over time allows contradictory ideas to be expressed. Obviously, the use of keywords is not limited to politics, but is to be found in other spheres of culture—as this discussion of sports, aesthetics and advertising has shown. What intrigues me is the fact that in Japan the same set of words crops up time and time again—almost like a ritual refrain—throughout society; it is not limited to any one sphere of culture. There is, then, a 'hard core' of keywords, numbering perhaps not more than a hundred, which seems to deal adequately with all aspects of Japanese culture.

In England, on the other hand, this does not appear to be the case. Keywords making up a vocabulary of evaluation certainly exist. But neither are the keywords of politics necessarily those of advertising, nor are the keywords of advertising usually those of aesthetics. The domains in which keywords are found are more or less separate. There is a 'hard core' of keywords in English society (democratic, right, individual, freedom, justice, classic, tradition, and so on), but in that their domain overlap is not so great as that of Japanese keywords, the hard core is smaller. At the same time, I would suggest that there is probably a greater number of less polysemic keywords used in English society, precisely because the domains of advertising, politics, sports, religion, aesthetics and so on do *not* overlap. This leads me to the following suggestion concerning the connection between keywords of evaluation and social organisation which, although tautologous, may have heuristic value; the greater the hard core of keywords, the more pervasive their existence in cultural domains and hence the more condensed their meaning.[6] This situation is characteristic of a close-knit social organisation such as is found in Japan. On the other hand, the smaller the hard core of keywords, the less their domain pervasiveness and semantic condensation. This situation is characteristic of a fairly loose-structured type of society, of which England and the United States are examples.

And so to my second conclusion. It can be seen, I think, that the argument about the role of the individual *vis-à-vis* the group among anthropologists dealing with Japan merely reflects the argument taking place in Japan's internal cultural debate. Not only this, but anthropologists dealing with Japan have long been accustomed to forming their own 'unique', closed-in social cliques. Hence we become not anthropologists, but Japanologists whose interests rarely coincide with what is deemed to be mainstream theory in anthropology. While there may be several explanations for this, and while we should not ignore the fact that Sinologists and Indianists may well feel out on a limb and yet still manage to contribute to anthropological theory, I suspect that every society to some extent dictates anthropology's approaches to it; it only allows us to study what it, the society, wants us to study, and so moulds us in its image. Hence I would suggest that anthropology itself ends up part and parcel of the internal cultural debate, both of the society being studied and of the society from which the anthropologist herself or himself comes. This is why perhaps anthropological theory will never be able to consist of a set of absolute, objective, scientific facts. Because it is closely bound by a continuing dialogue within and between cultures, theory can only consist of socially relative, subjective and—in that such theory can be said to be pleasing to one's sense of elaborated form—aesthetic intuitions. In short, anthropology is the 'mole' in the social science circus and we, its artists, smile at people's delusion.

Notes

1 Some might object to my using the words 'ritual' and 'rite' to describe a baseball competition, preferring alternatives like 'festival', 'performance', even 'cliche'. The sense in which I use the word is, however, akin to Barthes's *'mythologique'* (1972).
2 Friends have pointed out that after baseball games in the United States, announcers and camera teams go into the team locker rooms and ask each of the players how the game looked from short stop, left field, and so on. It is interesting that a nation which prides itself on 'individualism' should here focus on 'group' and team sports, while one that identifies with 'group' ideology should indulge in so many 'individualistic' sports (*sumō, kendō, jūdō, karate* and so on).
3 The ubiquitous victory-cum-congratulatory song played on such occasions in Japan is ironically the same tune as the Death March from Handel's oratorio *The Fall*. Charles Lamb later wrote a libretto for the tune, which includes the lines: 'Toll for the brave, the brave who are no more— / All sunk beneath the waves far from their native shore'. This supports the adage that the Japanese do not copy; they adapt!
4 *Kokoro* is cited 94 times in the *Kōkoku Bunan Jiten* advertising copy dictionary, published in 1980 by Senden Kaigi, Tokyo.
5 In fact, *kojinshugi* is probably rather close to the term *rikoshugi*, which means 'egoism'.
6 It is perhaps worth noting that cultural domains may be marked by social phenomena other than language. It is therefore possible for a number of domains to share the same evaluative keywords and yet remain distinct in the minds of actors through differences of, for example, dress, style, and purpose.

5

Negotiating aesthetics

Introduction

It will have become clear that in my discussion of tourism, high school baseball, advertising and aesthetics, I have moved from a micro- to macro-level study of language in society, from Ardener's Sociolinguistics *B* to *A*. One criticism of this latter approach could be that I have provided no ethnographic evidence to support interpretations that may well be nobody else's but my own. In order to allay such suspicions, therefore, I will in this chapter look at a different aspect of pottery aesthetics as they occur in the context of another popular cultural form—*mingei*, or folk crafts. Here I will once again write about those *sake*-drinking potters of Sarayama, Kyushu.

I have already made use of Parkin's notion of 'internal cultural debate' to focus on what I regard as an important, but hitherto neglected, aspect of linguistic usage in Japanese society. I now wish to take up his distinction between keywords (or 'invariable words' (1976)), and 'variable phrases', since it is through this distinction that new conventions become labelled and old ones relabelled or forgotten about entirely. Parkin's own interest was in the study of polygyny, bridewealth transactions and segmentary lineage organisation among the Luo in Kenya. He showed how, in public speech, keywords were used by those in power in an endeavour to maintain the *status quo*, while in private speech certain interest groups would make use of variable phrases in order to reinterpret the meaning of keywords. Precisely because keywords were conceptually condensed and lexically and syntactically predictable, it became possible to smuggle in new meanings. In other words, it was their conceptual ambivalence that allowed keywords to bring about change.

What I shall do in this chapter is discuss two ideals—one social, the other aesthetic—and then see how they work in practice. The social ideal is that advocated by Japanese sociologists and to a large extent by the Japanese people themselves. It focuses, as we have seen, on such concepts as 'harmony', 'co-operation', and 'selflessness'. The aesthetic ideal with which I shall here deal is that originally put forward by Yanagi Muneyoshi (or Sōetsu, as he later called himself) (1889–1961), founder of the Japanese folk craft (*mingei*) movement. It stresses that for folk crafts to be beautiful, they should be made with local natural materials in a spirit of co-operation and self-denial. The craftsman is expected to work in harmony with nature and not to be interested in financial gain. The aesthetic ideal therefore closely parallels the social ideal. The question is: what actually happens in everyday life? *Is* the Japanese individual so self-effacing and co-operative? *Do* people deny their 'selves' in order to appreciate 'beauty'? Is there any connection between the two ideals? Does a change in one, for example, affect the other? And how do craftsmen cope with such change? These questions I shall try to answer in the context of a pottery community that has found itself closely involved in the Japanese folk craft movement.

A model of community organisation

Although I have already talked about Sarayama (Onta) in Chapter 2, let me recap some of the basic details. The community lies near the north-western border of Oita Prefecture in central Kyushu. It is part of the hamlet of the same name and is situated within the administrative confines of Hita City (population: 65, 253 people; 17,573 households). About 17 kilometres from the town centre, it is located about 460 metres above sea level in the foothills of the Hiko-Gakumeki mountain range. These moutains effectively cut off Oita Prefecture from the north of Kyushu with its industrial urban complexes of Hakata (Fukuoka), Tobata, Yahata and Kokura.

Sarayama is as clean, as quiet, as physically attractive as most of Japan's cities are polluted, noisy and ugly. Situated in a narrow valley, which is hardly 200 metres across at its widest point, the community consists of just fourteen households. Of these, ten make pottery. Ever since it was founded in 1705, Sarayama has been almost completely isolated; it was only after the Pacific War that a road was put through to the community from the valley below. Its inhabitants were almost entirely self-sufficient; they grew their own rice and vegetables in land around the community. Pottery-making was a part-time job done by men when they had finished farming each day, or when the weather was too bad for them to work outside in the fields and mountains.

Since neither agriculture nor pottery-making could be managed by a single individual, in Sarayama—as in Japanese rural society in general—the household has been the fundamental unit of social organisation, with each individual first and foremost a member of his or her household. But each individual has also been a member of his community. In prewar days households in Sarayama were unable to take advantage of modern technology, and their work-force was insufficient to cope with certain aspects of production on their own. Consequently, each household was obliged to co-operate with others, not only for such agricultural tasks as the transplanting, harvesting and threshing of rice, but also for the digging of clays and glaze materials necessary to pottery. Like the household, the community was not simply a residential, but an economic group. Thus, ideally, the individual has been expected to subordinate his interests to those of the household and community to which he belongs; an individual participates in community activities only as a representative of his household (cf. Yoneyama 1967: 276); and relations between individuals have been effectively regarded as relations between households (cf. Fukutake 1967: 68, Nakane 1967: 125).

There are two particular aspects of the pottery production process in Sarayama that have contributed to a very strong sense of 'community solidarity'. One is the way in which clay has been prepared for use at the wheel; the other is the manner in which pots have been fired in a co-operative kiln.

In Sarayama, all pottery is made from a local clay which is rich in iron content and can be obtained from the nearby mountains. This clay is extremely hard. The only way it can be shaped at the wheel is if it is first powdered, then sifted and left to settle in tanks of water, before being dried. The rock-like substance of the clay means that something really heavy has to be used to break it into tiny granules and give the clay the plasticity the potter requires. In the days before modern machinery was devised to pound the clay (and adopted now, for instance, in the neighbouring pottery village of Koishiwara), water-powered clay crushers were the only means by which clay could be powdered effectively.

These clay crushers are usually found in groups of twos and threes, and line both mountain streams running through Sarayama. Water is channelled so that it flows into the hollowed-out scoop at the end of each crusher; the weight of the water makes the crusher see-saw down, empty the water from its scoop, and fall back with a thud onto a mound of clay placed under its far end. Each crusher has to be about fourteen feet long to be effective, and in order to see-saw properly, it has to be pivoted at a point about five or six feet from the tip of the hollowed-out scoop into which the river water pours. Each crusher, therefore, must be set at about the same distance above the bed of the stream from which it takes its water. As a result, there must be a drop between each crusher, or set of crushers. It is this which effectively limits the proliferation of households in Sarayama, for the total drop of the streams between the cultivated land at the top and that at the bottom of the community is fixed. Thus, the total number of households able to take up pottery in Sarayama is limited by the nature of the clay used to make that pottery.

A second point to be made about the use of these clay crushers concerns the composition of each potter household. The work-rate of each clay crusher, or set of crushers, is determined by the actual flow of water from the stream into the hollowed-out scoop at its end. The more water flowing through the two streams, the more frequently the crushers rise and fall; the more frequently they see-saw up and down, the more clay is prepared. Nevertheless, the flow of water is such that no potter household can prepare more clay than can comfortably be used by two men working full-time at the wheel. In other words, the nature of the clay and the method used to prepare it determine the composition of each potter household, in that the household head and only one son may work at throwing pots full-time.

The existence of the co-operative kiln has also had important consequences for Sarayama's social organisation. After pots have been made on the wheel, they have to be dried; then they are glazed and fired to a suitable temperature (about 1250° C). While there are various types of kiln suitable for firing stoneware-type pottery, in Sarayama potters have always used multi-chambered climbing kilns. Until recently, they chose to fire their pots in the same kiln, allocating each household an equal share of chamber-space in it. The fact that households sharing a co-operative kiln had to fire together meant that ultimately they were all tied to a similar work pattern. Thus, households found it expedient to dig their raw and slip clays, feldspar and iron oxide together, prepare wood and straw ash for their glazes together, and occasionally fetch down wood together to fuel their climbing kiln. Households co-operated with one another because they shared firings of the co-operative kiln.

Moreover, because potters fired their pots together in a kiln whose chamber-space was equally distributed, membership of the co-operative kiln also ensured that the economic standing of all households remained more or less the same. It was impossible for those living in Sarayama to rank households categorically accord-ing to wealth. Thus, the existence of this type of kiln has been responsible, not only for co-operation among potter households, but also for the egalitarian nature of that co-operation. Ultimately, it has given those living in Sarayama a remarkable sense of com-munity solidarity.

The Japanese folk-craft aesthetic ideal

So much for the social ideal. Let us now shift attention to the Japanese folk-craft (or *mingei*) ideal which acts as an aesthetic guideline for Sarayama's potters in the production of their work. The Japanese folk-craft movement was founded in the mid-1920s by Yanagi Muneyoshi. Yanagi was a philosopher and critic, who became interested in what he termed *mingei* (literally, 'popular art') for the way in which it accorded with his ideals of beauty. He proceeded to publish a series of essays in which he argued that, ideally, folk-crafts (as he liked to translate *mingei* into English) were 'beautiful' because they consisted of functional utensils made for everyday use by craftsmen who produced things cheaply and in quantity, relying on traditional methods of production and on the use of natural (as opposed to chemical or synthetic) materials. Folk-crafts were 'unpretentious', 'pure' and 'simple', made not by individual self-conscious 'artists', but by 'unknown craftsmen' who worked in co-operation with one another, unaware of the beauty of their work, untainted by motivation for profit.

According to Yanagi, the only way to appreciate 'beauty' was by using what he called 'direct perception' (*chokkan*). He argued that one had to put aside all concepts from the mind, to enter into a thing and see it for what it was—'directly' (Yanagi 1932: 56). Direct perception was 'beyond the self' (Yanagi 1955: 8) and was an ability to see crafts without the intrusion of subjectivity and all its possible prejudices. It was a method of aesthetic appreciation that defied logical explanation, denied artistic 'creativity' and was applicable by *anyone* (regardless of education or upbringing). 'Good' and 'beautiful' folk crafts could be recognised by anyone, provided that she made use of direct perception. Yanagi argued that if *chokkan* was 'subjective' or 'arbitrary', then it was not 'direct' perception as such (Yanagi 1954: 27–8).

Yanagi was convinced that his 'non-concept' of *chokkan* provided an aesthetic standard by which beauty could be unfailingly apprehended. Yet, for the most part, his theories were concerned with *how* folk-crafts were made, rather than with these crafts as objects in *themselves*. Provided that they were made according to a set of rules laid down by himself, they would naturally accord with his concept of beauty. These rules included the ideas that: (1) the craftsman should rely both environmentally and 'spiritually' on nature; he had to use locally obtainable materials and 'surrender his self' to beauty; (2) beauty should be 'communal', brought about by 'co-operation' and 'love'; (3) there was a close connection between the incentive for profit and the quality of the craftsman's work; (4) it was impossible for 'bad' craftwork to be born of a 'good' society (and in a good society the individual worked in harmony with others); (5) the beauty of folk crafts lay in their use—the more they were used, the more beautiful they became—and in this they differed from the purely decorative arts. We will come back to each of these points when examining the social changes which have taken place in Sarayama—primarily as a result of the Japanese folk-craft movement itself.

Yanagi originally 'discovered' Sarayama's pottery in 1927. When he actually visisted the community four years later, he was immediately convinced that these craft potters were the perfect example of his aesthetic theory of *mingei*. He wrote about them in local newspapers and in his monthly magazine *Kōgei* ('Crafts'), praising Sarayama's pottery because it had always been functional, rather than decorative. Potters were ordinary craftsmen who had no pretnetions to fame—simply people whose work was clearly lacking self-consciousness. The community of potters and their work were 'all tradition', unchanging since the first kiln had been fired in 1705. They were also 'close to nature', clay was prepared and pounded by water-powered clay crushers; pots were thrown on a kick wheel, dried in the sun, then glazed with local raw materials and fired in a wood-fuelled climbing kiln. All this was 'natural': modern machinery was not used at all (Yanagi 1931: 6–11).

Scholars and critics have, over the years, especially praised two aspects of pottery production in Sarayama. One is the fact that potters rely on natural methods of making and firing their pots; the other is that they work together as a group. Sarayama's pottery is 'beautiful' because potters help one another, theirs is a traditional way of life which is seen to derive entirely from nature. At the same time, nature affects a man's character and thereby the quality of his pots.

So, leaders of the folk-craft movement have praised Sarayama because they see potters as living in a kind of 'ecological equilibrium', in harmony with nature and with themselves. Yet, it is at this point that the first of a series of paradoxes occurs. By the late 1950s, Yanagi's ideas had become widely known and had caught on with the general public. Because Sarayama's pottery was regarded as beautiful and truly *mingei* in character, many people suddenly wanted to buy pieces made in the community. Visitors flocked to see the potters at work; most went as tourists, but for a significant few the trip to Sarayama has been a kind of pilgrimage, because the community and its pottery epitomise in their minds Yanagi's ideals of what 'true' folk crafts should be.

It is this growth in consumer demand that has been responsible for changes in the potters' social organisation during the past twenty years. Potters have found that they can now sell whatever they make. The less time they spend preparing their materials, the more pots they can throw; the more they throw, the greater their income. Farming ceases to be economically viable and co-operation breaks down; status differentials develop, based on wealth and talent; community solidarity is effectively undermined. Yet, precisely because potters adopt one or two technological innovations and stop working together, precisely because they begin to make a lot of money and their individual talent is recognised, folk-craft leaders then exclaim that the quality of Sarayama's pottery is rapidly 'deteriorating'. The social and aesthetic ideals end up as mutually destructive.

Aesthetic appreciation and problems of production

There are three general factors that have affected Sarayama's social organisation since the beginning of what is now known as the '*mingei* boom' of the mid-1950s. These are (1) technological innovations, (2) improved communications, and (3) increased market demand. Let us examine each of these in turn, and see how the aesthetic appreciation of Onta's pottery hinges on such changes.

The most important of the technological innovations concerns the way in which pots have been fired in the co-operative climbing kiln. In the old days, each chamber of the climbing kiln consisted simply of a sandy slope on which pots were piled fairly haphazardly. They could not be stacked very high, and most of the available space in a chamber was consequently wasted. However, in the 1950s, the technique of mass-producing strong, heat-resistant kiln shelving was developed. In 1959, one of Sarayama's potters bought some of these shelves and erected them in his allotted space in the co-operatively fired kiln.

The use of shelving had two major consequences, so far as production was concerned: firstly, the whole—and not just one third—of a chamber could be filled with pots, without fear of their falling over; secondly, it allowed the firing of a large quantity of small pots, which hitherto had not been made in Sarayama. The economic advantages of kiln shelving were not lost on the other potters, and by 1962 all potters in Sarayama had fitted the old sand-sloped chambers with shelves.

But the adoption of kiln shelving also affected Sarayama's social organisation, since it induced potters to spend their time on pottery rather than on agriculture. Kiln shelves made it technically feasible for potters to meet the enormous and new urban demand for small domestic wares. But to fill this demand, potters had to spend five or six times longer working at the wheel. Hence, from the early 1960s, both father *and* son in each household began to devote their time fully to wheel-work, rather than to farming as they had done hitherto. This decision was hastened by the Japanese government's adoption of a rice curtailment policy. Potters were not growing rice as a cash crop. Thanks to the introduction of kiln shelving, they were able to satisfy a continually increasing demand for their work. They therefore decided to give up farming.

Full-time specialisation in pottery production by ten out of Sarayama's fourteen households has led to a breakdown in community solidarity in a number of ways. First of all, co-operation among households in such agricultural tasks as the transplanting and harvesting of rice came to an end. Moreover, because potters purchased ball mills to prepare certain glaze materials, households stopped pooling their labour for such tasks as pounding straw ash. This breakdown in co-operation was exacerbated by a general improvement in communications in the 1960s. With the widening and metalling of country roads, potters found that they could get their materials by car, or in some cases have them delivered to Sarayama. Whereas, in the past, each houshold had had to spend fifty-five man-days per annum cutting wood for the kilns, or thirty-six days a year digging clay, by the end of the 1960s wood was being delivered ready-cut from lumber yards in the neighbouring town of Hita, and a bulldozer was hired to dig clay for the potters once every three years. The time that each household had spent on the acquisition and preparation of pottery materials was reduced by more than two-thirds. Every potter could now devote more than two additional months a year working full-time at the wheel.

It was, of course, the sustained demand for folk-craft pottery that was the underlying force behind these changes. Potters adopted kiln shelving and purchased ball mills because it made economic sense to do so. They thought it worth their while to alter their methods of production, so they hired a bulldozer to dig their clay, they ordered by telephone slip clay for their decorating and wood to fire their pots. It was no longer necessary to continue farming because there was market demand for their pottery.

But this market demand led to potters' ceasing to co-operate with one another and to their relying on the use of money to conduct their everyday lives. In other words, the use of cash gave rise to impersonal relations. Potters have become extremely wealthy. Within the space of fifteen years, their incomes have jumped from an average of ¥600,000 (£2,750) a year to just over ¥8,000,000 (£37,000) a year. It is perhaps not surprising to find that several potters have attempted to maximise their economic gains by building privately-owned kilns. They can then fire their pots at as fast a rate as they please, without having to participate in the co-operative kiln system, where they must wait for slower potters to complete their quota of pots before firing. Thus, the co-operative kiln, which was originally shared by all potting households, is now fired by only five.

As mentioned earlier, the co-operative kiln effectively limited and standardised all potters' incomes and gave rise to financial equality within the comunity of Sarayama. Now that half the potters have built their own kilns and fire independently, they have widely varying incomes. At the same time, market demand also gives potters incomes far exceeding those of non-potting households. As a result, households in Sarayama are beginning to be ranked hierarchically according to criteria of wealth. Notions of 'equality' and 'community solidarity' have been further upset.

In addition to these social consequences of technological innovations, improved communications and a sustained increase in consumer demand, there are also aesthetic consequences for Sarayama's potters. As we have seen earlier, Japanese folk-craft leaders have a very clear perception of what the craftsman's relationship to his environment ought to be. Thus, any discrepancy between this 'cognised' model and the actual 'operational' model (Rappaport 1971: 247) leads to severe criticism. In general, folk-craft beauty has been seen to disappear with the onslaught of

Western civilisation. It is said that *mingei* kilns have been 'ruined' by material changes which upset man's relation to 'nature'—by, for example, the substitution of charcoal or oil for wood in the firing of kilns; by the use of plaster moulds or jigger and jolly, rather than kick wheel, to form pots; and by the inclusion of chemical substances instead of natural materials in glaze compositions (*cf.* Mizuo 1966: 83).

Not surprisingly, perhaps, Sarayama's pottery has been to some extent criticised as a result of the technological and social changes that have occurred in the community. Critics argue that the adoption of kiln shelving, and the consequent change in chamber-loading methods, have led to poorer results in the slipware. It has also been suggested that the quality of the wares has suffered because potters now buy wood ash from the lumber yards instead of making it themselves, and because they purchase slip clay from distant Arita, rather than dig it from the mountains around the community (*cf.* T. Tanaka 1961: 8; Y. Tanaka 1965: 24). Potters have also had to contend with the argument that their work has 'deteriorated' because they have stopped farming and because a bus now plies between Hita and Sarayama, bringing with it tourists who are interested only in 'superficially beautiful' pots (*cf.* Hamada 1965: 9; Miyake in *Nihon no Mingei* 190: 7; Tanaka Takashi 1969: 47; and B. Leach in conversation). Onta pots are seen to be 'polluted' (Mizuo 1968: 110).

Further criticism of Sarayama's pottery stems from the fact that potters now earn so much money. It is frequently asserted that the richer potters become, the more their work deteriorates. Potters are seen to put profit before quality in their hierarchy of values, and this can only lead to further 'pollution' in their work (Mizuo 1971: 61; *cf.* Yanagi 1955: 128–30). With the increase in the demand for folk crafts, critics say that Sarayama's pottery is losing its qualities of 'craftsmanship' and 'healthy pricing'. It has moved away from the essence of *mingei*, away from its original 'beauty' and 'honesty'. Those craftsmen who wish to survive have to make the choice between what are seen as two evils: to become individual artist-craftsmen and produce something more closely approximating 'art', or to turn out mere souvenir items that will inevitably be classed as a form of 'ethnokitsch' (Mizuo 1966: 84–5).

Changes in methods of production, therefore, have had a number of adverse 'aesthetic' effects on the quality of Sarayama's pottery. In addition, community solidarity is being further weakened by certain marketing practices and by the appreciation of pottery by those living outside Sarayama. Methods of retail pricing, of promoting potters' names and of exhibiting pottery, all serve to emphasise the potter as an individual, rather than as a member of his household or community.

With regard to retail pricing, first of all, shop owners and dealers fix their prices according to the quality of the pots that they hope to sell. They also have to take current market considerations into account. However, when a buyer decides that one pot may be better than another, he is in fact suggesting that one potter may be superior to another. Any differentiation in price ends up as a differentiation in individual talent.

Buyers are interested in good pots because they are made by good potters. Buyers' profits can be increased if they are able to 'sell' the potter. They therefore encourage customers to buy the products of certain potters whose work they stock and whose individual names they do their best to promote. What buyers do not realise—and what potters theoretically cannot accept—is that within the sphere of the hamlet group all households must be more or less equal. If one potter is consistently picked out for what outsiders see as 'good' work, he and his household are going to gain status, and hence destroy the ideally non-ranking equilibrium of all households in Sarayama. By promoting the names of certain potters, and by pricing their work higher wherever possible, buyers are threatening the solidarity of the community. Thus, within Sarayama, individual talent has to be denied unless it reflects upon the community as a whole.

And yet potters cannot ignore their buyers entirely, for they do, after all, have to make a living. They therefore comply—albeit unwillingly—with requests to sign their names on some of their pots, particularly those that are to be used in the tea ceremony or given as 'personalised' presents at a wedding or other such function.

Ironically, in view of the fact that folk crafts are supposed to be made by 'unknown craftsmen,' it is the folk-craft associations themselves that have been largely responsible for the publicizing of Sarayama's potters' names. Both the Japan Folk-Craft Association (*Nihon Mingei Kyōkai*) and the Japan Folk-Craft Society (*Nihon Mingei Kyōdan*) hold annual autumn exhibitions in their museums in Tokyo and Osaka respectively. Sarayama potters are asked to send in their work to these exhibitions, and almost every year some of them are awarded prizes. Moreover, in 1973 potters were encouraged to contribute to a biannual national exhibition known as the Japan Ceramics Exhibition (*Nihon Tōgeiten*). Although only two potters did so, one of them was promptly awarded one of the four major prizes at the exhibition.

The news of this potter's success astonished everyone in Sarayama, and the media paid so much attention to him that his name became extremely well known amongst those interested in pottery and folk-crafts. But such attention only served to affect even further the concept of 'community solidarity' in Sarayama. There was some resentment among the potters, as their prize-winning comrade was called upon by outside forces to act as spokesman for internal affairs when he was still a comparatively young man in his mid-30s. (The appointment of the potters' official spokesman—the cooperative leader—was based on seniority in age.) Thus, public evaluation of a single pot did not just lead to acclamation of the individual who made that pot; it also conflicted with the seniority system prevalent in the conmmunity in which the individual concerned was living.

This was not the only occasion on which the Folk-Craft Association's dealings with potters upset the community's gerontocracy. In 1962, one of the employees of Yanagi's Folk-Craft Museum was sent to stay in Sarayama and advise potters concerning what was, and what was not 'acceptable' *mingei* pottery. Over a period of ten years, the lady concerned continued to come down from Tokyo, staying a few days at a time in Sarayama, talking to potters and making suggestions concerning the shapes, decoration and glazing of certain pots. Understandably, some of the older potters began to resent her appearance in the community, since she posed a threat to the hitherto unquestioned assumption that the way they taught their sons to pot was the best possible way. As a result, she found herself naturally associating with those potters whose fathers were not working with them at the wheel. This resentment may have been the inevitable result of the existence of Sarayama's household system, but it led to the Folk-Craft Association publicly approving the work of younger potters. Such approval merely served further to weaken the community's system of gerontocracy. It has also made it possible that potter households will be ranked in the future in terms of talent—and not just wealth—if the appraisal of Onta pottery continues in this manner.

Direct perception and an aesthetic standard

Earlier on, when examining the ideology of the folk-craft movement, we saw that Yanagi was mainly interested in beauty and that what he called 'direct perception' was, in his opinion, the only means of understanding 'true' beauty. He argued that, in aesthetic appraisal, one had to rid the mind of all concepts and allow a thing to be seen and to 'speak' for itself. Direct perception gave rise to a *standard* of beauty which could be appreciated by anyone, regardless of education or upbringing.

During my fieldwork, I questioned both Sarayama potters and folk-craft leaders about this point. Their reaction was extremely interesting. All of the dealers and many of the potters felt that direct perception was not simply an abstract theoretical concept, but one which could be successfully practised. In other words, they accepted the idea that one should try to see a pot for what it was—'directly'. However, neither dealers nor potters were prepared to accept that direct perception could provide a *standard* of beauty. The reason for their disagreement with Yanagi on this point stemmed from their own experiences in selling pottery. Potters, for example, often found that what they regarded as excellent work, dealers or the general public would ignore entirely; what they thought were rather poor pots, on the other hand, were frequently the first to be sold after a kiln firing.

The general opinion of both potters and buyers was that there had to be, and was, individual interpretation in people's decisions as to what was, and what was not 'beautiful'. They argued that, if there was an overall standard of beauty which could be shared by anyone using direct perception, everyone would in theory end up buying the same pots. This, in fact, did not happen. Potters and buyers were therefore convinced that direct perception could only provide a personal, *subjective* standard of beauty. The appreciation of beauty depended entirely on the individual.

This point is of interest in that it shows how the aesthetic appraisal of folk crafts parallels the social practice of the potters' ideal of 'community'. We have seen that, in the social organisation of Sarayama, *ideally* the individual is not as important as the primary group to which he belongs—in other words, to the household or hamlet in Japanese rural society. *In fact,* however, the marketing of pottery has made the household more important than the community, and the individual more important (to outsiders at least) than the household. The individual does not always put group interests first; he can, and does, manipulate group ideals to his own personal advantage. The social ideal is not matched by social practice.

Similarly, according to folk-craft *theory,* the determination and understanding of 'beauty' is neither arbitrary nor subjective. If a man 'surrenders his self', he can create beauty; if he rids himself of prejudice and uses 'direct perception' (what Bourdieu (1984: 1–7) refers to as the 'pure gaze'), he can appreciate beauty. But potters and buyers argue that *in practice* the appreciation of beauty is always individually oriented, and that what is beautiful for one person is not necessarily so for another. Thus the aesthetic ideal is not matched by aesthetic practice either.

Negotiating words

What we have seen in this description of Sarayama's pottery community is that potters, critics, buyers and, to some extent, the general public, are all using a fixed 'aesthetic' vocabulary with which to negotiate their positions within the context of the folk craft, or *mingei,* movement. Indeed, the word '*mingei*' itself caused some difficulty. Critics for their part were concerned that the concept's *philosophical,* or moral, content not be in any way 'contaminated'. They thus adopted a different attitude from buyers, on the one hand, who used *mingei* because it helped *sell* pots, and from potters, on the other, who felt that the word had come to broaden and change in meaning so much since its inception in the mid-1920s that they would have preferred that the term not be used at all of their *community*.

For all this difference of opinion, the word '*mingei*' itself served to maintain a dialogue between the members of this somewhat disparate trio. The same can be said of '*kokoro*', much discussed in the previous chapter. Although in some respects the notion of a craftsman's 'heart' is nullified by the rarefied selflessness of what Yanagi called the 'self-surrender' (*tarikidō*) to *chokkan*, the beauty of folk crafts did depend to a large extent upon the craftsman's spiritual attitude, as seen in his 'love' for his work, his ability to co-operate with others, and in his 'unlearned' (*mugaku*) unself-consciousness. In fact every potter did believe that handicrafts expressed the craftsman's character and that they were, to one extent therefore, imbued with *kokoro*. What they did not accept, however, was the idea that beauty was born *solely* from the craftsman's 'heart'. They added—and this point echoes their criticism of direct perception—that what they saw in one of their pots and what a critic or buyer saw in the same pot were very different.

In this context we should realise that the notion of *kokoro* is, of course, closely connected to that of '*shizen*', or nature. Yanagi argued that the environment in which the craftsman lived and worked was vital to the quality of folk crafts, whose beauty he saw as depending largely on the craftsman's 'closeness to nature'. This was only partly accepted by the potters, for a number of reasons. Firstly, they did not agree that their work was good *because* they relied on natural materials and on natural methods of production. Other potters could fire their wares in gas kilns and prepare their clay with pug mills and still make good pots. Secondly, they were not convinced that either they—or, more importantly, the critics—could distinguish between the 'natural' and 'unnatural' elements of a finished pot (wood-fired *vis-à-vis* gas-fired pots; natural *vis-à-vis* chemical glazes; kick *vis-à-vis* electric wheel thrown pots). They did support the equation between 'nature' and 'beauty' in folk crafts, but only because Sarayama is virtually the only pottery kiln in Japan still relying almost totally on 'nature' in its production. For potters, 'nature' set the *community* apart.

Dealers were adamant in their opinion that there was an aesthetic connection between nature and beauty. Some even said that Onta pottery would go to the dogs if potters started using mechanical methods of preparing clay and gas- or oil-fired kilns. What buyers really meant here was that they would be unable to sell Onta pots as effectively as hitherto, if production methods changed to those practised by other potters throughout Japan. In other words, as far as dealers were concerned, 'nature' set the *pottery* apart.

There was also a close association in both dealers' and critics' minds between a man's spiritual attitude, the nature of the environment in which he lived, and the quality of the work he produced. In particular, they envisaged the craftsman as living in secluded, beautiful surroundings undisturbed by the bustle and noise of urban life. In actual fact, this was hardly the case: potters were constantly interrupted by tourists and other visitors; they spent most of their time 'drowning' the silence outside with their radios, and one young man actually threw all his pots at the wheel while watching television! To the rural craftsman, nature is not something to be contemplated aesthetically in a detached manner. Rather, it is the environment in which he works; it is 'the source of his success and of his fears' (Tomars 1940: 390).

Clearly, people idealise nature only when they are not directly involved with it in a struggle for survival. In other words, the aesthetic ideal that associates the quality of folk crafts with closeness to nature derives primarily from urbanisation and, of course, from industrialisation (upon which urbanisation usually—though not necessarily—depends)—a point to which I shall return in Chapter 10. In one sense, then, the idea of an aesthetic theory centring on the concept of beauty may be said to derive from the destruction of nature which has hitherto accompanied urbanisation.

Not only this, but people who bought Japanese folk crafts used the concept of 'nature'—perhaps unconsciously—as a means of measuring just how far Japanese culture has progressed (*cf.* Graburn 1976: 13–14). They believed not only that the potters of Sarayama made good pots *because* they used natural materials and means of production, but that potters *ought* to continue to rely on nature and not yield to economic considerations. The moral tone found in Yanagi's concept of nature, and adopted by present folk-craft leaders, would appear to extend to a large section of the Japanese public. Potters in Sarayama work in a way in which almost the whole of Japanese society once worked; now that Japanese industry has made such advances, people like to look back and see how far they have progressed. They want potters in Sarayama to stay the way they are, so that they can measure their own and the nation's prosperity. In exchange, they are prepared to accord potters the 'honour' of acclaiming their work as 'art' (see Moeran 1984: 223–230).

Conclusion

I have in this chapter tried to lay bare the underlying semiotics of Japanese folk crafts, and to show that there is an intimate relation between social and so-called 'aesthetic' ideals in the pottery community of Sarayama. We have seen, first of all, how social organisation has been affected by various changes in the community's relation to its natural environment; and secondly, how it has been further upset by potters' contacts with the outside world. Such changes in Sarayama's social organisation have also affected the critical appraisal of the potters' work by leaders of the Japanese folk craft movement. Thus, failure by potters to meet a social ideal becomes simultaneously a failure to meet an aesthetic ideal. Any social change necessitates a corresponding change in aesthetic appraisal, because of the close parallel between it and the social ideal of how *mingei* should be made. If potters remain 'close to nature', their work 'improves'; if they fail to co-operate, their work 'deteriorates'.

Now, it may be asked to what extent *mingei* is typical of other popular cultural forms. My answer would be that *structurally* it is no different from such artistic pursuits as the tea ceremony or *ikebana* flower arrangement. Each of these has created an ideology which—like *mingei*—centres on such precepts as 'denial of the self', 'anti-intellectualism', and 'harmony with nature'. And yet it is clear that the practice of both the tea ceremony and *ikebana* involves their adherents in a set of social relationships (notably, the pyramid-like relations between teacher and pupils, known as the *iemoto* system), which can seriously undermine the apparent 'purity' of aesthetic ideals. This is not surprising. As I have argued elsewhere (Moeran 1987), the practice of *every* art form involves a clash between aesthetic, commodity, and social values. Indeed, it may well be this clash that ultimately defines something as 'art' in the first place. Here what is of interest is the fact that so called 'aesthetic' ideals are in fact no more, and no less, than prescriptions for the organisation of Japanese society. *Mingei, ikebana*, the tea ceremony—each is in this sense, perhaps, the 'autobiography of society' (Mukerjee 1948: 57).

6

Californian car-lore

Introduction

We have now examined the way in which the meanings of words can be negotiated. What we have not yet done is look at how they get introduced into people's vocabulary in the first place. In this chapter, therefore, I want to follow the possible means by which Japanese words get exported and taken up by those living abroad. In this way, I should be able to show that popular cultural forms are not as innocent as they might at first glance seem.

A few years ago, while doing research in and around Sarayama, I became intrigued by the way in which certain 'non-indigenous' cultural elements came to be adopted by my neighbours in the country valley in which we lived. My initial awareness of the problem started when I was obliged to build a stone wall to shore up a somewhat precipitous slope below our house. At the end of three days' backbreaking work, I realised that I had built a European wall, consisting of square or rectangular stones which I had laid in overlapping layers as though they were bricks. This wall was very different from the other walls which formed the stepped rice paddies in the valley, and which consisted of round or rhomboidshaped stones dropped into one another in a manner totally different from my own brick-laying style.

This was not the only element of local 'culture' which will doubtless cause one or two puzzled archaeologists to scratch their heads in a few hundred years' time. In the same valley—and only, so far as I know, in this one valley—a number of farmers' wives grew dillweed. Apparently, dill had been brought there by men who had been imprisoned in Siberia and had learned about the herb's uses from the Russians. They thus referred to dillweed as *roshiagusa,* or 'Russian grass' (Moeran 1985b: 158, 228).

A few years ago, when I was invited to teach at the University of California, Berkeley, my attention was attracted by the vogue for personalised number plates on cars and trucks. In order to while away hours made idle by the sheer size of the university campus, I used to note down in my pedestrian travels those number plates that struck me as especially intriguing or amusing. Some I found peculiarly 'Californian'—like LIF LOVR, for example, or JOGNLIV, EVERHI and GODSINU. Others made dextrous use of the fact that environmental licence plates (as the personalised plates are officially called by the Department of Motor Vehicles in Sacramento) were limited to a combination of seven letters and/or numbers: PCOFMND (Peace of Mind), MCMLXV (the year of the car's make), GN2LNCH, XCLNT and TPLZ BNY (Topless Bunny, for a Volkswagen *Rabbit* Hatchback). Yet others were little more than onomatopoeic sounds for the cars they licensed: VVVVVVV, RUUUMMM, and ZZZOOOM.

I soon noticed that a number of Japanese words occurred among the environmental license plates. Many of these were clearly the names of car owners—as in IMYURI, SUMISAN and MORIOKA; but many more included words and phrases which were used by and known to both American and Japanese-American car owners. Although a full list of such license plates would be tedious, many of them do take on significance in my discussion of language and popular culture, and it is these that I shall outline here.

Nature, culture and art

We have already seen that nature plays an important part in Japanese aesthetics. It was perhaps not surprising, therefore, to find that a number of car licence plates referred to various aspects of nature. Thus I came across SHIZEN (Nature), and MIDORI (Green[ery]), along with YAMA (Mountain), YUKI (Snow), and SORA (Sky). Astronomical bodies included TA YO (Sun), TSUKI (Moon) and HOSHI (Star), while flora and fauna were represented by HANA (Flower), UME (Plum), FUJI (Wistaria (or possibly, Mount Fuji)), SAKURA (Cherry), KIKU (Chrysanthemum) and MOMO (Peach).[1] In general, birds and animals were not found, although exceptions included TSURU (Crane) and TSUBAME (Swallow), symbols of long life and prosperity respectively. HEBI (Snake) was seen on an AC Cobra, and BEARSAN on a car owned by a student who supported the 'Golden Bears' football team of the University of California, Berkeley.

Artistic activities were frequently represented, too: HAIKU and KABUKI, IKEBANA and CHANOYU (Tea Ceremony), not to mention the ubiquitous GEISHA. At the same time, many of the aesthetic concepts associated with the practice of such arts were also found: BI (Beauty), AWARE (Pathos), SHIBUI (Subdued, Quiet), IKI (Chic), YUGEN (Quiet Beauty), and MUJO (Impermanence). Given the 'religious' significance of one or two of these terms, together with a West Coast predilection for Asian religions, it was perhaps not surprising to come across MATSURI (Festival), DAIMOKU (Prayer Chanting) and any number of variants on ZEN—ZENBIKR, ZENCAT, ZENMIND, ZENMOBL, ZENZERO, and ZAZEN. To these should be added the linguistic puns, ZENEMY (The Enemy) and ZENXOUS (Zen Anxious).

As a philosophy, of course, Zen Buddhist thought has been associated with other popular cultural forms such as the martial arts: AIKIDO, JUJITSU (together with its variant JUJUTSU), KARATE, and KENDO. The changes were rung on JUDO, too, with JUDOKA, JUDOFUN, and JUDOMOM, while the SAMURAI code of BUSHIDO made an appearance, together with BUSHI (Warrior) and NINJA (Acrobatic Spy). Not to be outdone, SUMO had such variations as SUMOIT, I SUMO, and SUMOCAR.

All such activities, whether cultural or martial arts, emphasise the importance of their mode of instruction, so that it was hardly surprising to find SENSEI (Teacher) and DESHI (Pupil) on number plates. Other traditional social roles included OYABUN (Patron) and KOBUN (Client), together with those types of person generally associated with feudal-like relations: DAIMYO (Feudal Lord), SHOGUN, and YAKUZA (Gangster).[2]

Family relations were also frequent: ONNA (Woman) and OTOKO (Man), together with KODOMO (Child), OTOSAN/OTOSAMA (Father), OKASAN (Mother), ONISAN/NISAN (Elder Brother), OJISAN/OJICHAN (Uncle), OBASAN/OBACHAN (Aunt), and OJIISAN (Grandfather). Marital ties could be seen in SHUJIN (Husband), TSUMA, OKUSAN, and YOME (all meaning Wife), while the whole concept of continuing generations of the Japanese household occurred in DAIDAI.

Over the past two decades, Westerners have shown increasing interest in Japanese popular cultural forms—particularly, perhaps, in fashion and clothing. It was thus hardly surprising to come across GETA, HAPPI/HAPPII, KIMONO, and OBI, since these are the items almost invariably depicted by Westerners trying to realise their images of Japan. Food and drink, however, also received attention, with GOHAN (Boiled Rice), SEKIHAN (Congratulatory Red Bean Rice), TEMPURA (Deep Fry), PAN (Bread) and the somewhat unexpected NINJIN (Carrot). Other foods included the ever popular SASHIMI, together with at least a dozen variants of SUSHI, while thirst quenchers included ASAHI, KIRIN, and SAPPORO beers, together with the more traditional SAKE and its toast of KAMPAI or KANPAI.

Car-lore and keywords

The ideas contained in the car licence plates decribed here are not simply mirrored in popular cultural forms. Many of them reflected the kind of Japanese 'spirit' discussed in previous chapters. KOKORO (Heart) was one such example; MUSHIN (No Mind), WA (Harmony), and TAMASHI (Soul) were others. More words characteristic of the 'group model' of Japanese society include: GIRI (Social obligation), NINJO (Human spontaneity), SHINNEN (Conviction), SHINBO (Perseverance), KONKI (Endurance), ANTEI (Established), KONJO (Disposition), SHOJIKI (Honesty), MAKOTO (Sincerity), and JISHIN (Self-confidence).

There was, however, a second group of words which directly contrasted with this sense of 'Japaneseness', revealing instead an idiosyncracy, or KOSEI, more characteristic of what might be seen as a 'fun-loving', 'Californian' way of life. These included OKASHII (Funny), URESHII (Happy), KIREI (Attractive), HEIKI (Self-possessed), NONKI (Easy-going), KAKKOII or KAKKO E (Groovy), and SUTEKI (Marvellous). More down to earth were ZURUI (Crafty), SUKEBE (Lecherous), ETCHY (Dirty-Minded), and BAKA (Fool). These last words came in for a number of variants, as did KOI (Love, or Carp).[3] Thus I came across such neologisms as BAKABOY, KOIJOY, ETCHYS, KOINUT, BAKASAN, and KOIFISH.

Now it seems to me that we have here a variation on the opposition that we encountered when we looked at the language of high school baseball, pottery aesthetics and advertising slogans: two groups of words representing two different aspects of Japanese culture. Here I would argue that the first group is probably close in 'spirit' to the *formal* aspects of Japanese culture spread abroad. It consists of words which are compatible with the ideals of the martial arts, for example, and of Japanese art in general, and which—along with cuisine and fashion—reflect the acceptable face of Japanese 'tradition' as it is propagated both at home and overseas. Californian car-lore here accords with the dominant ideology.

The second group of words is not part of the 'official' mainstream cultural tradition of Japan. Although such words are frequently used in Japan, they tend to be frowned upon by those in authority since, as we have seen, they express a certain 'individuality' and suggest that Japanese society might be moving away from its traditional values towards a modern and 'Western' system of morals. In this respect, the second group of words provides an *informal* counter-balance to the almost 'religious' character of the words listed in the first group.

Linguistic and cultural innovations

I began this chapter by referring to two examples of cultural contact in a remote valley in central Kyushu. In the first, the story about a brick-like wall, a Western way of doing things was practised by a Westerner living in a Japanese community. In the second, the story about the origin of *roshiagusa*, local Japanese brought back from a Western society a herb which had not hitherto been used or grown in their own community. At the moment, there is no evidence to show that Japanese living in the valley concerned are likely to adopt my method of constructing stone walls. Still, there is, I suppose, the chance that at some stage in the future they might see fit to do so, for some wives now successfully grow beetroot from the seeds that we have given them, while others have wholeheartedly adopted my wife's method of making *yomogi*, or 'mugwort', bread which they sell in the local supermarket.

Given the present importance of the Japanese economy, it is not surprising to find that a large number of words and phrases are becoming assimilated into English. 'Workaholic' is an everyday phrase that has no need of italics, while *sōgō sōsha, shinpan* and *shuntō* are now being used to refer to trading companies, consumer credit companies and the annual spring wage-bargaining offensive by magazines such as *The Economist*. In the meantime, the *Walkman* has come to relieve those obliged to spend an unanticipated length of time at the mercy of British Rail, and people can now participate in annual *karaoke* competitions in London pubs.

Brick walls and dillweed are just two examples of the way in which objects and artefacts have been converted into 'cultural' items in a remote Japanese valley. In a wider context, I would suggest that words frequently cross linguistic boundaries in a somewhat similar manner. In California, some environmental licence plates with Japanese words on them have probably been registered by members of Japanese immigrant families (the '*brick wall*' route); others by those living in California who have had some sort of contact with Japanese culture[4] (the '*dillweed*' route). Many more words are probably adopted as a result of mutual contact—in much the same way as my Japanese wife learned to make bread from some American neighbours in Kobe many years ago, proceeded to experiment with the ingredients, and then taught local Japanese farmers' wives how to make *yomogi pan* (the '*mugwort bread*' route).

Although considerable attention has been paid by both Japanese and Western scholars to the way in which Japanese has been borrowed from European languages, particularly from English, not many have addressed themselves to the way in which Japanese words have been adopted into (American) English. Nagara (1972) has considered the use of Japanese pidgin English in Hawaii, and Miller (1967: 256–9) has enumerated several words which have come into more or less general usage in the United States in particular. These include tycoon (*taikun*), *mikado*, and *hara-kiri*, together with a number of words connected with art (e.g. *shibui*), nature (e.g. *ginkgo*), food (e.g. *soy* sauce), and fashion (e.g. *kimono*).

Clearly, there is a tendency for vocabulary items connected with Japanese popular cultural forms to be adopted into American

English (and other Western languages). The arts, food, and fashion are, after all, three of the more exportable aspects of culture in general (as our own Gallicised vocabulary reveals). This point is supported by the number of such words found on Californian environmental licence plates—IKEBANA, CHANOYU, AWARE, SHIBUI, ZEN, JUDO, SUMO, KARATE, SUSHI, SASHIMI, SAKE, OBI, GETA, KIMONO, and possibly HAPPI.[5] Here the 'brick wall' route has been prominent, as the Japanese themselves introduce their own language into the society to which they have migrated over the past century or so.

Other words, however, are less easy to classify. SUKOSH and SUKOSHI (meaning 'a little'), for example, could well be a hangover from post-war *pangurishi*, or 'street walker English', picked up by those employed in the American military during Japan's occupation after the Pacific War (Miller 1967: 263). The fact that the spelling of this word is usually abbreviated—as in a fashion ad, *'a skosh more tight at the hips'*—shows just how much this Japanese loanword has been assimilated into the American-English phonetic system. Other words on Californian licence plates that would also seem to stem from 'bamboo' or 'street walker' English included DAIJOBU, DAIICHI DAISUKI and TAKUSAN. Loanwords like these have almost certainly been brought into California (and the United States) by the 'dillweed' route.

Now if, as I have here suggested, a number of keywords involving formal aspects of Japanese culture, particularly those connected with popular cultural forms, *have* been borrowed into (American) English by the 'mugwort bread', rather than 'brick wall' or 'dillweed', routes of cultural assimilation, Californian environmental licence plates form an interesting antithesis to the tourist brochures discussed earlier. As I see it, the 'mugwort bread' type of loanword is the flip side of the tourist coin spun into the air in Chapter 3. International tourism not only threatens the ideals of Japanese society; it allows these very ideals to permeate those of other cultures and, when backed by the full weight of media ignorance (as is the case with Western exposition of the group model of Japanese society), promotes a splendid brand of 'orientalism'. Who ever said that either language or popular culture was innocent?

Notes

1 In view of the fact that licence plates included KIKUYO, KIKUKO, MOMOE, and MOMOCAR, it could well be that some of these names were of car owners, rather than of natural species.

2 The success of the television series *Shōgun* may well have been responsible for ANJIN 2 (Pilot two/too).

3 *Koi*'s connotations of both 'love' and 'carp' have been neatly combined in a London car bumper sticker: *Carp Society members do it for love!*

4 This was the case with one of my U.C.B. students who had lived in Japan and rode around in a convertible with KAKKO E on it.

5 I say 'possibly' because HAPPI may very well be a mis-spelling of 'happy' (*cf.* the licence plate HAPPI 2B).

7

The poetics of advertising

Introduction

Enough has been said about words in the past few chapters, I think, to have pressed home the point made earlier: that *semantic* categories are vital to any discussion of a people's perceptions and world view. In this respect, my approach has differed somewhat from the classical application of the Whorfian hypothesis, for example, which focuses on *grammatical structures*. I do not wish to deny totally, however, the importance of grammar to an understanding of the way in which the Japanese perceive things, and so, in the following three chapters on advertising language, I will focus more on general linguistic structures. By comparing the slogans of Japanese and British advertising, I hope to point out some of the similarities and differences in the language usage of two societies that have taken more or less the same long and winding road of industrial capitalism.

This particular chapter starts out from an article by George Milner (1971), who noted that a number of Samoan proverbs were to be found in the form of distichs, and that in fact traditional sayings all over the world tended to fall not only into two matching halves, but also into matching quarters (like *More haste, less speed,* for example). He suggested that one feature of such sayings was that they had a quadripartite balance, based on both syntactical and semantic factors. From this initial insight, Milner proceeded to set out a number of types of syntactic parallelism and to show that these were accompanied by certain types of semantic structure.

While cycling around the streets of London on my way to and from university (in the years—not so long ago—when I still had the energy for such activity), I noticed that there was a tendency for British advertising slogans to take on forms of syntactic and semantic parallelism similar to those described by Milner. I then began leafing through the dozens of weekly and monthly Japanese magazines donated me by businessmen starved of news from home while posted out 'in the sticks' of a north European capital, only to discover that very few of their advertisements had the same kind of quadripartite structure I was looking for. There were some, it was true; but not that many. And yet quite a few of their proverbs—like *Gō ni ireba, gō ni shitagae* ('When in Rome, do as the Romans') or *Isseki nichō* ('Two birds with one stone')— obeyed Milner's hypothesis. This struck me as odd. If British advertising slogans were proverbial in form, and if the structure of proverbs was universal, regardless of the different structures of the languages in which such proverbs were phrased, then why did so few of the Japanese advertisements that I saw have the kind of syntactic and semantic parallelism noted by Milner?

Quadripartite structured advertising slogans

Before trying to answer this question, let me give my readers some examples of what I am talking about. As I have already intimated, a large number of English advertising slogans are to be found in the form of distichs. For example:

For Daily Quality (4)
Take the Quality Daily

The luxury car is dead (40)
Long live the luxury car

(Numbers in parentheses refer to the Appendix.)

That advertising companies consciously recognise such slogans as forming distichs can be seen in the way that they frequently set them out in two parts—either horizontally, as in:

Less smoke   More heat (29)

or vertically,

Remember last winter? (41)
Don't forget this

103

or in blocks,

Born in	*Raised in*	(15)
Denmark	*Britain*	

As with traditional sayings and proverbs like *More haste, less speed*, or *Spare the rod, spoil the child*, many advertising slogans' distichs are made up of two distinct portions of roughly equal length and balancing each other. In other words, each matching half has a matching quarter. This quadripartite balance is due partly to syntactic and partly to semantic factors, and it is this parallelism which can be said to give such slogans much of their effect.

Syntactic symmetry is often complete. For instance, two adjectives may be found, joined by a conjunction in each half of a distich:

> *Long and slender* (16)
> *Light and mellow*

Or a verb phrase may be followed by a noun phrase in each distich:

> *Regardez la qualité* (19)
> *Comparez les prix*

Or a main verb phrase is preceded, or followed, by a subordinate verb phrase in each distich:

> *As a biochemist, I recommend Skin Dynamics* (3)
> *As a woman, I love Skin Dynamics*

> *Why give a collector's item that barely lights up the room* (37)
> *When you can give one that brightens up the holidays?*

Other combinations of verbs, adjectives and nouns giving syntactic symmetry are also found:

> *After giving you more on the ground* (5)
> *We're giving you more in the air*

> *Long on resources* (28)
> *Short on red tape*

> *If you don't ask for the lager you want* (46)
> *Don't be surprised at the lager you get*

Milner (1971: 245–6) distinguishes four types of semantic parallelism accompanying syntactic symmetry:

(1) Two contrasted and antithetical statements which stress contradictions, make comparisons, or point to reciprocal or complementary activities:

Instead of chipping away at your savings   (33)
The government is actually chipping in

Style. It's hard to define   (35)
But easy to recognize

(2) Two paratactical statements which often stress the same point and reinforce each other:

Discover du Maurier   (1)
Discover low tar

No FT . . .   (48)
No comment

(3) Two conjectural statements with a premiss or hypothesis in the first half, followed by a conclusion in the second:

The longer you smoke   (8)
The more you'll like Kool Superlongs

If it isn't smooth   (47)
It isn't Smirnoff

(4) Two consequential statements, in which an event or cause is stated in the first half of the distich and its alleged or predicted result in the second:

When prohibition hit Southern Comfort   (31)
New Orleans discovered the blues

Because Sony redesigned the car stereo   (44)
The automakers don't have to redesign the car

Milner categorised Samoan sayings by giving each quarter a plus (+) or minus (−) marking according to whether it contained a 'good' (desirable, useful, safe, friendly, valuable, attractive) or 'bad' (undersirable, useless, dangerous, hostile, despised, unattractive) referent. He was thus able to establish four main classes of quadripartite saying, each divided into four subclasses (which were not significant). I have done the same for a selection of English and Japanese advertising slogans (see Appendix).

What emerges from an analysis of fifty English advertising slogans is a conclusion which most of us as consumers would take for granted. Quadripartite structured slogans are likely to be adopted only when they express positive, rather than negative, values. Furthermore, advertisers appear to favour slogans which, if they are to include negative values at all, end up on a positive note in the second half of the distich. There are thirty-one examples in the A, and ten in the B, groups, but only nine in the remaining two groups put together. So far as the internal structure of the slogans is concerned, twenty have positive markings in both head and tail of each half of a distich; thirteen have positive markings in all but one quarter of the distichs; and sixteen have an equal proportion of positive and negative markings. Only one of the slogans analysed had three or more negative markings in its quadripartite structure.

Advertisers' preference for positive, rather than negative, values has already been noted in another context by Leech (1966: 153), when he listed the ten adjectives most frequently used in English advertising: 'The high frequency of *good/better/best* contrasts with a very low frequency of its antonym *bad/worse/worst*. In fact, against nearly a hundred occurrences of *good* there was not a single instance of *bad* in direct address in the television sample. If *bad* is avoided, the pejorative counterparts of adjectives of more enthusiastic praise (*ghastly, dreadful, etc* as opposed to *wonderful, delicious, etc.*) are even less likely.' It can be seen, therefore, that a preference for certain meanings gives rise to a preference for certain forms of syntactic structure.

In his study of traditional sayings of Samoa, Milner (1971: 247) argued that within each half of a quadripartite saying, 'the two quarters have independent values which modify and affect each other, but do not modify the quarters of the other half'. The point about advertising slogans is that it is precisely the relation between the two halves, and not just their quarters, which is vital to our understanding of them. Pateman (1983: 188–90) has pointed out that almost invariably we identify advertisements as such *in context* and bring to our understanding thereof at least *some* knowledge of the language and culture involved. Hence, a strictly formal analysis of the linguistic structure of a slogan cannot of itself lead to an understanding of the message being communicated.

Let me try to clarify this point by citing a few examples. When we hear someone in England talking about Polo mints, we know that a particular type of mint-tasting sweet is being referred to: it is circular and has a hole in the middle. When we read an advertisement for Polo mints, therefore, which goes:

Even when the mints have gone (49)
The holes are still there

we give the word *holes* a meaning that it would not normally have in other contexts. That is to say, it does not allude simply to the 'hole in the heart' feeling of despondency we tend to have at the end of something pleasant; rather, the fact that Polo is the 'mint with the hole' suggests to us that even when the mint in question has been sucked into annihilation, the flavour of Polo lasts for ever, precisely because the holes remain. We interpret the word *holes* therefore, in a *positive* way *across* the two halves of the distich, but in a *negative* way *within* the second half of the slogan.

Another example of the way in which our knowledge of the context of advertising affects our interpretation of the slogan used is:

When prohibition hit Southern Comfort (31)
New Orleans discovered the blues

Within the second half of the distich, we can see that the discovery of the blues is a positive value so far as New Orleans and American culture are concerned. However, across the two halves of the distich, we immediately assume that the effect of the inhabitants of New Orleans being deprived of their alcohol was to make them feel 'blue'. *Blues* thus takes on a negative value.

The point, then, that I wish to make about advertising slogans is that their full meaning only becomes clear when they are read across, as well as within, each half of their distichs. It is this which enables us to make the leap from car to house design in:

Sitting room at the front (18)
Spare room at the back

and from a regal drink to typically British weather in:

In Denmark it reigns (42)
In Britain it pours

It is, then, precisely the spatial economy in slogans of this type, where certain words and phrases say one thing while suggesting another, which gives the quadripartite structure in advertising copy its force.

> Quick to reach 60 (23)
> Slow to grow old

> Forget that she's your wife (30)
> Remember she's a woman

> If you aren't getting More (50)
> You're getting less

Japanese advertising slogans

If we turn now to examine Japanese advertising slogans, what do we find? Does Milner's hypothesis hold true? The short answer to his question is 'yes'. Some—though not many—slogans in Japanese do follow the quadripartite pattern; they make use of similar forms of syntactic parallelism to those noted above and they tend to stress positive, rather than negative, values (see Appendix).

> asa wa seiji ni (J1)
> kumo wa jiki ni natta
> The morning has turned to celadon
> The clouds to porcelain

> monogatari no owari wa (J11)
> monogatari no hajimari da to shiru
> It's known that the end of a story
> Is the beginning of a story

> sedan dakara (J15)
> sedan na no ni
> Because it's a sedan
> In spite of its being a sedan

> sekushii dake wa, kanashii yo (J17)
> yasashii dake wa, sabishii yo
> Sad just to be sexy
> Lonely just to be tender

There is, however, a longer answer to Milner's hypothesis. This runs: 'yes, some slogans are formed with quadripartite structures, but in general the quadripartite structure in Japanese advertising copy is not a *preferred* form of presenting material'. You would not expect to find in Japan, for example, someone adding a graffiti to a billboard slogan in such a way that it forms a quadripartite structure with the original advertisement:

> *If it were a lady, it would get its bottom pinched* (Fiat 127)
> *If this lady was a car, she'd run you down* (Anonymous)

Moreover, the Japanese slogans which are found in the form of distichs rarely match their English counterparts in syntactical complexity. For instance, I have yet to come across an example of the kind of chiastic structure found in:

> *Because we don't touch anything but the bacon* (45)
> *There's no bacon to touch ours*

and rarely do the Japanese slogans extend beyond the simplest syntactical forms:

> *Good taimingu* (J6)
> *Good kyashingu*
> *Good timing*
> *Good cashing*

> *furesshu na kaori* (J2)
> *sawayaka na nodogoshi*
> *A fresh fragrance*
> *Cool in the throat*

There is, however, one aspect in which Japanese distichs *are* more complex than English quadripartite slogans and that is in their use of Chinese characters. Very often, the parallelism and opposition between each half of a distich derives almost entirely from the juxtaposition of contrasting Chinese characters. This means that it is possible to argue that quadripartite slogans in Japanese may be distinguished *visually* as well as syntactically. Thus, in the first example, there is a contrast between the characters *su* (素) and *bi* (美); and, in the second, between *reki* (歷) and *tō* (陶).

> *sugao wa* (J5)
> *bigao da*
> *One's face as it is*
> *Is a smiling face.*

> *hitokuchi rekizen* (J7)
> *futakuchi tōzen*
> *One mouthful, obviously*
> *Two mouthfuls, gloriously drunk*

That this form of parallelism is consciously, rather than fortuitously, created can be seen in:

mizu ga aru	水がある	(J8)
kōri ga aru	氷がある	
We've got water		
We've got ice		

where the addition of one stroke of the character for 'water' (*mizu*) gives 'ice' (*kōri*); and in another advertisement by the same whisky company:

hi ga aru	火がある	(J9)
hito ga iru	人がいる	
We've got fire		
We've got people		

where the erasing of two strokes from the character for 'fire' (*hi*) leaves us with 'man/people' (*hito*).

This means that the Japanese language provides advertisers with a form of parallelism not generally available to users of English. Moreover, the fact that Japanese can be written in the Roman alphabet, and two 'indigenous' syllabaries, besides the Chinese characters, means that advertisers are able to set up further oppositions through combinations of *rōmaji* (the Roman alphabet), *hiragana* and *katakana* (the two Japanese syllabaries).

The nearest that English advertisers can get to this sort of parallelism is by changing a single letter in one half of a distich, as in:

First over	(7)
First ever	

or by conscious use of alliteration. For example:

Wrought from pure silver
Writes like pure silk

The poetic function of advertising slogans

So much for the data. At the beginning of this chapter, I posed a question which I must now try to answer: why should the quadripartite structured slogan be a preferred form for British advertisers, but not for Japanese?

One approach, of course, could be that of the Sapir–Whorf hypothesis again. After all, English is an Indo-European language, while Japanese is probably part of the Altaic group (Miller 1967); the two languages differ considerably in their grammatical structures.[1] The fact that English and Japanese advertising slogans clearly opt for different structures of meaning, therefore, might well encourage those who argue that what distinguishes the Japanese from Westerners (or Chinese) is that the Japanese do not make 'a rigid distinction between modes of thought and structures of sentiment, between rationality and non rationality, or between logos and pathos' (Nagashima 1973: 111).

Nevertheless, given the differences in the structure of the two languages concerned, speakers of English would be expected to differ from speakers of Japanese in the way that they think about experience. Not that this solves the problem, of course. The fact that there is a difference in the way people express experience does not prove that the experience itself is not the same—a point missed by Kumon (1982) when he distinguishes between a Western cognitive process, which is 'comprehensive' in the way it moves from individual elements to a larger whole, and a Japanese cognitive process which is 'analytical', in that it starts with the whole before dividing it up into smaller parts.

Rather than tie myself up in theoretical knots (and hence be reduced to the kind of sado-masochistic bondage that typifies the *eroduction* films I shall be discussing in Chapter 11), I would prefer to leave aside the Whorfian hypothesis and consider a second, possibly more fruitful, proposition. In an essay devoted to the relation between linguistics and poetics, Jakobson (1960) has suggested that there are six different functions of language—referential, emotive, conative, phatic, metalingual and poetic—one of which will predominate in any verbal communication, depending on the emphasis placed on context, addresser, addressee, contact, code, or message, respectively.[2] The poetic (or 'aesthetic' (Mukarovsky 1976)) function, according to Jakobson, is most noticeable when emphasis is placed on the message for its own sake, and it is characteristic of verbal art. By this he did not wish to imply that the poetic function is *only* to be found in poetry; rather, it exists in verse-like messages, such as mnemonic lines (*Thirty days hath September*), modern advertising jingles, and versified medieval laws. 'All these metrical texts make use of poetic function without, however, assigning to the function the coercing, determining role it carries in poetry' (Jakobson 1960: 359).

Clearly, advertising slogans in general are marked by a number of features peculiar to the poetic function, and I would suggest that it is the difference between the poetic functions of messages in English and of those in Japanese which can be said to account for the reason why the quadripartite slogan is a preferred form in English, but not in Japanese, advertising. This difference I see as consisting of an emphasis on alliteration, assonance and structural completeness in English, as against a preference for association, suggestion and structural incompleteness in Japanese. By this I do not mean to imply that assonance, for example, is totally alien to the Japanese, or association to the English, poetic function; rather, that some features are more marked than others, and that it is these marked features which appear in advertising slogans. In short, Japanese advertisers do not make use of the quadripartite slogan as a preferred form because the poetic function of verbal communication in Japanese does not emphasise phonological or metrical symmetry. Rather, it stresses an 'aesthetic of suggestion' (Keene 1972) in which words of association express an 'undercurrent of meaning' (Jakobson 1960: 373).

It is entirely possible, of course, that Japan's wholesale adoption of Western culture is affecting the way in which the Japanese express experience. This is a point that I have touched upon before in my discussion of the 'language of modernity'. In which case it may be that, with time, Japanese advertisers will move away from the traditional poetic function of their own language and adopt instead features of the poetic function of English in particular. If this does happen, we can expect a marked increase in the usage of quadripartite slogans and in the complexity of their structure.

Appendix: Outline of a scheme for the classification of quadripartite advertising slogans

1 English examples
In the first class (A), all four subclasses have a positive head and a positive tail.

A1:

1

Discover du Maurier +
  +   +
Discover low tar +
  +   +

du Maurier

2 High gear
  Low gear

Adidas

3 As a biochemist, I recommend Skin
  Dynamics
  As a woman, I love Skin Dynamics

Skin Dynamics

4 For Daily Quality
  Take the Quality Daily

Daily Telegraph

5 After giving you more on the ground
  We're giving you more in the air

Air France

6 Great bitter
  Great value

Toby Ale

7 First over
  First ever

Philippine Airlines

8 The longer you smoke
  The more you'll like

Kool Superlongs

9 From the dawn of the world
  To the ends of the earth

PIA

10 Big enough for the family
   Fast enough for the boys

Mitsubishi Colt

11 The elegance is obvious
   The excellence is rare

Seiko Lassale

12 When the occasion arises
   Only one sherry rises to it

Harvey's Bristol Cream

13 The new Parker arrows
   The same old Parker aims

Parker Arrow

14 The Danish can
   The British do

15 Born in Denmark
   Raised in Britain   *Carlsberg*

16 Long and slender
   Light and mellow   *Kim*

17 From shaggy sheep with a sense of
   style—
   From Scotcade with a sense of value   *Samband of Iceland, Hekla*

18 Sitting room at the front
   Spare room at the back   *Vauxhall Carlton*

19 Regardez la qualité
   Comparez les prix

20 Regardez l'élégance
   Comparez les prix   *Cristal d'Arques*

A2:
(No examples of this subclass, in which all quarters are marked negative.)

A3:
21

Fancy a jar?	+
+ +	
Forget the car	+
− −	

                                  DOE

22 It's well up to continental standards
   At well below continental prices   *Sherborne Fitted Kitchens*

23 Quick to reach 60
   Slow to grow old   *Volkswagen Scirocco*

24 Thinking of your bedroom,
   and double it . . .
   Think of a price, and halve it   *Acme Fitted Wardrobes*

25 When you make a great beer
   You don't have to make a great fuss   *Heineken*

26 More live contacts
   Fewer dead ends

27 More locations
    Fewer dislocations

28 Long on resources
    Short on red tape   *Standard Chartered Bank*

A4:
29

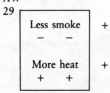

                                        Coalite

30 Forget that she's your wife
    Remember she's a woman   *De Beers*

31 When prohibition hit Southern Comfort
    New Orleans discovered the blues   *Southern Comfort*

In the second class (*B*), all four subclasses have a negative head and a positive tail.

B1:
(No examples of this subclass, in which quarters are marked + −/− −.)

B2:
(No examples of this subclass, in which quarters are marked − +/− −.)

B3:
32

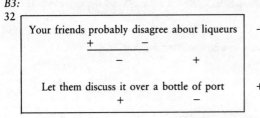

                                        Cockburn's

33_ Instead of chipping away at your savings
    The government is actually chipping in   *M & G Life*

34 Cold place
    Fire place   *Solid Fuel Advisory Service*

115

35 Style. It's hard to define
   But easy to recognize   *Morris Marina*

B4:
36

If an ad is wrong	−
+ −	
We're here to put it right	+
+ +	

                                           Advertising Standards Authority

37 Why give a collector's item that barely
   lights up the room
   When you can give one that brightens up
   the holidays?   *Tanqueray Gin*

38 Where you see obstacles
   We may see paths   *Dresdner Bank*

39 Times change,
   But Martell never varies   *Martell*

40 The luxury car is dead
   Long live the luxury car   *BMW*

41 Remember last winter?
   Don't forget this   *Bluecol*

In the third class (C), all four subclasses have a positive head and negative tail.

C1:
(No examples of this subclass, in which quarters are marked + +/− +.)

C2:
42

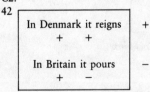

In Denmark it reigns	+
+ +	
In Britain it pours	−
+ −	

                                           Carlsberg

43 When the slopes are great
   The roads are rotten   *Eagle*

44 Because Sony redesigned the car stereo
   The automakers don't have to redesign
   the car   *Sony*

C3:
45

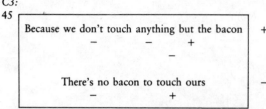

                                 Danepak

C4:
(No examples of this subclass, in which quarters are marked − −/+ −.)

In the fourth class (*D*), all four subclasses have a negative head and a negative tail.

D1:
(No examples of this subclass, in which quarters are marked + −/+ −.)

D2:
46

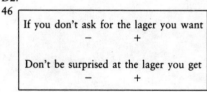

                                McEwan's

47 If it isn't smooth
   It isn't Smirnoff   *Smirnoff*

48 No FT ...
   No comment   *Financial Times*

D3:
49

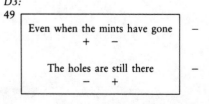

                                Polo

D4:
50

> If you aren't getting More   –
>   –   +
>
> You're getting less   –
>   +   –

More

2 Japanese examples
A1:
J1

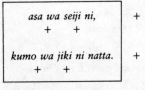

> *asa wa seiji ni,*   +
>   +   +
>
> *kumo wa jiki ni natta.*   +
>   +   +

Korean National Tourist Organisation

The morning has turned to celadon
The clouds to porcelain

J2 *furesshu na kaori*
   sawayaka na nodogoshi   *Hakushika Sake*
   A fresh fragrance
   Cool in the throat

J3 *oishisa wa, ayashisa*
   ayashisa wa, yasashisa   *Kyōwa Sainte Neige Wine*
   Taste is mystery
   Mystery is tenderness

J4 *supesharisuto de aritai, to omou*
   zenerarisuto de aritai, to mo omou   *Kanebō Eroica*
   I think I want to be a specialist
   I also think I want to be a generalist

J5 *sugao wa,*
   bigao da.
   One's face as it is   *Onward Fashion*
   Is a smiling face

J6 *Good taimingu*
   Good kyasshingu
   Good timing   *Seibu Credit*
   Good cashing

J7 *hitokuchi rekizen*
   futakuchi tōzen   *Seagram Crown Royal*
   One mouthful, obviously
   Two mouthfuls, gloriously drunk

J8 *mizu ga aru*
   kōri ga aru   *Suntory Old*
   We've got water
   We've got ice

J9 *hi ga aru*
   hito ga iru   *Suntory Old*
   We've got fire
   We've got people

J10 *ore wa umai kara nomu*
    watashi wa biyō no tame ni nomu   *Nihonshū Centre*
    I drink it because it tastes good
    I drink it to be beautiful

A2:
A3:
A4:
(No examples of these subclasses.)

B1:
B2:
B3:
(No examples of these subclasses.)

B4:
J11

monogatari no owari wa		–
+	–	
monogatari no hajimari da, to shiru		+
+	+	

Mazda Cosmo

It is known that the end of a story
Is the beginning of a story

J12 *kotton na no ni*
    kantan na no ne   *Toyobō Maycare*
    Even though it's cotton
    It's simple

119

C1:
J13

mitsumeru me + +	+
mitsumerareru me – +	–

Rodenstock

Eyes that gaze
Eyes that are gazed at

J14 *okuru koto ga yorokobi to nari*
okurareru koto ga hisoka na hokori to
naru   *Suntory Imperial*
Giving is a pleasure
Being given is a secret pride

C2:
J15

sedan dakara + +	+
sedan na no ni + –	–

Nissan Prairie

Because it's a sedan
Although it's a sedan

J16 *ikki*
ichiyū   *Ranman Sake*
One joy
One sorrow

C3:
C4:
(no examples of these subclasses.)

D1:
J17

sekushii dake wa, kanashii yo + –	–
Yasashii dake wa, sabishii yo + –	–

Trojan Daimaru

Sad just to be sexy
Lonely just to be tender

D2:
J18

otoko wa, onna ni jinsei o okuru
+   −   +   +
−   +
onna wa, otoko ni kōhaku-iro o okuru
−   +   +   +
−   +

−

−

Nikka Fortune '80

A man gives a woman his life
A woman gives a man the colour of
amber

D3:
D4:
(No examples of these subclasses.)

Notes

1 There are certain groups of people in Japan who go so far as to suggest that the Japanese language is in fact 'unique', unrelated to any other language in the Altaic group (Miller 1982).
2 Jakobson's argument in fact owes much to an earlier paper by his former colleague in the Prague Linguistic Circle, Jan Mukarovsky (1976 (originally 1936)), who himself refers back to Karl Buhler's model of the three basic functions of the linguistic sign.

8

The media mosaic

Introduction

If the structure of Japanese advertsiements is in some respects different from that of English advertisements, is there any way in which they can be said to be the same? Now, it is clear that advertisers the world over try to generate some form of discourse in their advertising slogans. In this respect, Berger (1972: 131) has argued persuasively that in the advertising of modern industrialised societies every image confirms and enhances every other. Publicity—as he refers to advertising—is thus not simply an assembly of competing message but a language in itself.

What are the characteristics of this language? Berger's own interest was in tracing parallels between the language of publicity and that of art, and he has shown how advertisers use art works and techniques to make their messages more effective. After all, 'unlike advertising, Art has a reputation for being above things vulgar and mercenary, a form eternal rather than social, whose appreciation springs from the discerning heart, not the cultural background' (Williamson 1987: 67), so that advertising uses art as an ideology to mask its determining aim of profit (Haug 1986: 129). All kinds of strategies of art are expropriated to create a style, as advertisers—representatives of that high cultural elite— seek to impose their aesthetic vision on the consumer masses (Marchand 1985: 117–63). We have already seen that this 'aesthetic vision' can be linguistic as well as pictorial. In Chapter 4, I argued that advertisements are at the heart of what might be called an 'internal cultural debate' (or, in more fashionable parlance, 'discourse') in contemporary Japanese society.

In the following two chapters, then, I wish to compare British and Japanese advertisements in order to see in what form this so-called discourse takes place. My argument will be that, while there are numerous parallels between the two cultures in the way in which their advertising slogans allude to and parody other forms of media communication, they differ sharply in their linguistic form. Specifically, whereas the language of English advertising would appear to prefer to play on *grammatical* structures (along the lines of the verbal play often practised in black American urban communities and generally known as 'sounding'), Japanese slogans are more likely to focus on *lexical* items, which then become 'keywords' in the advertising discourse.

The media mosaic and 'cultural knowledge'

One of the results of advertising in both England and Japan is that its slogans are often regenerated into popular sayings in their own right. English soccer fans, for example, owe their laudatory *Nice one, Cyril!* to a Wonderloaf Bread slogan, while *We aim to please* is a catchphrase that started with newspaper ads and brochures in travel agencies and employment bureaux.

Similarly, in Japan, housewives' *Sappari shiteru kara, suki* ('I like it because it's plain and simple') originated in a catchphrase for Marina margarine, and the popular *Hawaii e ikō* ('Let's go to Hawaii') comes from a Suntory *Torisu* whisky advertisement. Other slogans that have filtered into everyday speech include the Japan Tobacco Monopoly's *Kyō mo genki de, tabako ga umai* ('Feeling well today, too, and tobacco tasting good'), Gon Insecticide's *Teishu genki de, rusu ga yoi* ('My husband well and out of the house'), and *ganbare Gensan* ('Stick to it, Gen')—a slogan for a health food to help students pass their exams.

More frequently, of course, it is conversational clichés and adages that are taken up by advertisers and used as slogans, generally in some form of pun. Just a few recent examples from English advertising include:

Tall, dark and have some (Guinness)
All the fun of the share (Quality Street)
Fast. But not furious (Mazda)
The stuff that drams are made of (Grant)

Cyclists should be seen and not hurt (Greater London Council)
Just what the dentist ordered (Mentadent)
Go on, pull the other one (Pepsi)

Similar word games are played by Japanese advertisers, who make full use of proverbs as they indulge in what—as we might expect from examples in the previous chapter—are frequently visual, as well as phonetic, puns. An English proverb, *Time is money*, makes its appearance with *Toki wa en nari* ('Time is *yen*', Mitsubishi Bank), while *Haya oki wa 3 sai no toku* ('The early riser gains three years', Sony) plays on a Japanese proverb that refers to the connection between time and money: *haya oki wa 3 mon no toku* ('The early riser gains three pence'). This notion of hard work being rewarded crops up again in Akadama port wine's *Akadama ni oitsuku byōki nashi* ('Sickness is a stranger to Akadama'), a slogan which plays on *kasegu ni oitsuku bimbō nashi* ('Poverty is a stranger to industry'). *Baka to hasami wa tsukaiyō* ('Fools and scissors make good servants') is parodied by Heibonsha's *hyakka to hasami wa tsukaiyō* ('Encyclopaedias and scissors make good servants'), while Nissho Iwai's *Atsusa, samusa mo tobira made* ('Hot, then cold, then hot again until the door') takes off *atsusa, samusa mo higan made* ('Hot, then cold, then hot again until the autumn equinox').[1]

Popular sayings or phrases are also frequently used. Maipi Liner's *Shirigami kōkan* ('Bottom paper change') plays on the cry of the street vendor who collects old newspapers for recycling and gives toilet paper in exchange (*Chirigami kōkan*). Isetan Department Store's *Nekutai rōdō* ('Tie Labour') puns on the 'workaholic' ethic of physical labour (*nikutai rōdō*), while, in *Oyabin kobin* ('Parent bottle, child bottle'), Suntory Orange substitutes 'bottle' for 'part' in the well-known 'parent-child' (*oyabun kobun*) relation of patronage practised in certain spheres of Japanese society.

Japanese advertisements also play on English. *This Izu* (Japan National Railways) recalls the first sentence ever learned by Japanese teenagers at school ('This is a pen'), while *How are yu* (Tokyo Gas) needs no further explanation. In each case, the English words 'is' and 'you' are replaced by Chinese characters for 'Izu' (a place name) and 'hot water' respectively. In a similar vein, English advertisers have been known to practise a form of pidgin French. For example:

Parlez-vous petroleum (Phillips Petroleum)
C'est bargain (Sally Ferries)
Le crunchtime (French Golden Delicious)[2]

This form of 'sounding' on what might be termed 'cultural knowledge' often alludes to various aspects of the media. Not only are popular sayings reinforced by their occurrence (albeit as puns) in advertising slogans, but advertisers make use of popular books, films, television programmes, theatre, music and so on to reinforce a cultural knowledge on which advertisers can then draw in order to further their cultural discourse.

Since advertising is 'a highly organised and professional system of magical inducements and satisfactions' (Williams 1980: 185), it is hardly surprising to find English slogans alluding to the magical world of children' fairy tales. Benedictine uses the slogan *It turns a frog into a prince*.[3] Foster's makes a joke of the fact that it brews an Australian lager with *The Wizard of Oz*. In Japan, a Hans Christian Andersen tale of a mermaid princess is parodied by Toshiba in its commercial for the new *Walky* (*Odoroki/momo no ki/uōkī*), while a well-known phrase, *E ni mo kakenai utsukushisa* ('Undepictable beauty'), from a similar type of fairy tale—involving Urashima Tarō and a Dragon Palace princess—is alluded to by Kadokawa Novels in *E ni mo kakenai omoshirosa* ('Undepictable interest'). In *Kaze no Matasaburō*, the drug company Ruru puns on the fact that *kaze* can mean 'cold' as well as 'wind' in the name of a children's story character created by Miyazawa Kanji. Ōzeki takes the ghost story *Banchō sara yashiki* ('The haunted house of plates')—in which the maid, Kiku, is put to death for breaking a lord's precious plate and returns every night to count them one by one—and changes it to the 'haunted house of *sake*' (*Banchō sake yashiki*), in which the maid's voice counts up the new 'one cup' glasses of *sake* drunk by the protagonist.

Modern fairy tales, of course, are often filmed, rather than written. As a result, it is no surprise to discover that advertising slogans can allude both to the film industry and the works that it produces.

Fly Delta. The official airline of Walt Disney world (Delta)
How to get to Hollywood via a brief appearance in Dallas (American Airlines)

Butch, ring Sundance (British Telecom)
The French connection (Pirelli)
From Here To Eternity (Nike)

Here the Japanese are particularly prolific. The never fading charisma of Marilyn Monroe is found in *Kaerazaru kasa* ('Umbrella Of No Return', Tokyo Metropolitan Subway), while Leonard Bernstein's musical *West Side Story* occurs in Keio's *Uesuto saizu sutori* and Hanpen's *Uesuto saizu monogatari* ('Waist Size Story'). Print Gokko prefers a more modern sci-fi film with *2001-nen purinto gokko no tabi* ('2001—A Print Gokko Odyssey'), but Westerns remain ever popular, as can be seen in:

Babachizoku no saigo (Johnson)
The Last of the 'Babache' Germs

Shēnu kamubakku (National Panacolor Video)
Shane, Come Back!

Kaette kita ganman (Daimaru)
The Return of the Gunman

Makaroni isetan (Isetan)
Macaroni 'Eastern'

In the past, directors have frequently moved from commercials to cinema and then ignored their training ground in cinematic techniques. (Ken Russell, for example, is said to have gone from Shredded Wheat to *The Music Lovers*). Nowadays, though, famous directors do not necessarily see commercials as being beneath them. The director of *Fatal attraction*, Adrian Lyne, has made commercials for Special K and Ford, while Hugh Hudson, of *Chariots of Fire*, has helped sell Fiat Strada. It is perhaps not surprising to find, therefore, that a large number of television commercials now parody famous films. Recent examples in England include the *Blade Runner* spectacular run by Barclay's Bank in an attempt to promote deposit accounts; a sequence from *Brief Encounter* used to sell a Birdseye frozen dinner; parodies of Raymond Chandler films encouraging consumers to drink Tennants lager; the chariot race from *Ben Hur* designed to exemplify Audi's *vorsprung durch technik*; and the Eerie Lackawana train scene from *Starlight Express* in which a Woody Allen look-alike gazes mournfully at a packet of KP Nuts.

Japanese advertisers are also prone to 'sounding' off Western

films. We find *Bonnie and Clyde* scenes (*They're young ...
They're in love ... And they kill people*) being used by Lion
(Emeron) in a series of advertisements for dandruff shampoo; the
marriage scene from *The Graduate* (*Sounds of Silence*) transferred
to a Japanese shrine by Nisso (*Wakame! Menkoku!*); look-alikes
of Marilyn Monroe (*Mannekin Monroe*—Hotel Juraku), Hum-
phrey Bogart (*Otoko no mune wa, Casablanca*—Canon), Alain
Delon and Charles Bronson (*Saraba tomo yo*—Isetan); a romantic
scene from *Love Is A Many Splendoured Thing* in Hong Kong
adopted by Ajinomoto; *Stagecoach* in full flight, chased by a
Mitsubishi *Mirage*; and a combination of *Goldfinger* and *For
Your Eyes Only* to advertise the Mitsubishi *New Canter* (*0090
Gold Canter*).

At the same time, Japanese advertisers make sure to draw on
their own cinematic traditions. 'Noodle western' *samurai* films
(which I shall be looking at more closely in Chapter 10) are
parodied in advertisements by Momoya (*Chūshingura, Miyamoto
Musashi*); Gin'ō (*Sanbiki no samurai*); Barusan (*Takeda Shingen*'s
battle flag *furin kazan*); Renown and Hakugen (*Kurama Tengu*);
while *yakuza* gangster heroes are idolised in commercials by Mitsubishi Rayon (*Tōei ninkyō eiga*); Edo Murasaki (*Kogarashi Mon-
jirō*); Momoya and Hakugen (*Kunisada Chūji*).

A number of film slogans, such as Mazda's *How the West will
be won* and de Beers' *A diamond is forever*, derive from literature,
and Japanese advertising, too, makes full use of its literary herit-
age. The dreaded athlete's foot (*mizumushi*), which tends to afflict
people during Japan's humid summer months, is described in the
following terms by Lisboa:

> *Haru wa akebono. Yō yō kayuku nariyuku. Natsu wa mizumushi. Tabi no
> koro wa saranari.*
> In spring the dawn. As the itch creeps in ... In summer athlete's foot.
> Especially when travelling ...

Any Japanese would recognise this as a parody of the famous
opening passage of Sei Shōnagon's *Pillow Book* (*Makura no
sōshi*):

> *Haru wa akebono. Yō yō shiroku nariyuku yamagiwa sukoshi akarite murasa-
> kidachitaru kumo no hosoku tanabikitaru.*
> *Natsu wa yoru ...*

> In spring [it is] the dawn [that is most beautiful]. As the light creeps over the hills, their outlines are dyed a faint red and wisps of purplish cloud trail over them.
>
>   In summer the nights ... (Morris 1970: 21)

A seventeen-syllable *haiku* by Bashō in his *Narrow Road to the Far North (Oku no hosomichi)* suffers no better a fate:

> *Shizukesa ya/wa ni shimiiru/semi no koe*
> Stillness—seeping into the rock, the voice of a cicada

is transformed into:

> *Shizukesa ya, tēpu ni shimiiru hito no koe* (National)
> Stillness—seeping into the tape, the voice of a person

And to the photograph of two Tarzan and Jane-like figures in the jungle by a portable tape recorder is added the phrase 'Grand Nature' (*dai shizen*).[4]

Another famous poem concerns the character of the first Tokugawa shogun, Ieyasu, and his two predecessors, Oda Nobunaga and Toyotomi Hideyoshi. When asked how they would make a 'canary' (*hototogisu*) sing, Nobunaga is said to have replied that he would 'kill it' (*Koroshite miyo*), and Hideyoshi that he would 'make it sing' (*nakasete miyo*). According to legend, however, Ieyasu said merely that he would 'wait until it sang' (*Nakazunba/ naku made mato/hototogisu*). In an attempt to restrain its passengers from overcrowding its rush hour trains, the Tokyo Subway Corporation suggested that they *Okorazu ni/tsugi made mato* ('Without getting annoyed, wait until the next [train]'), and included a picture of the three feudal warlords adopting different postures on a station platform in order to press home the analogy.

Other literary puns include *Hyakunin isshu*—the title of a famous collection of poetry compiled by Fujiwara Sadaie in 1235, in which the character for *shu* (首) (a poem counter) is changed to *shu* (酒), '*sake*', by Suntory; *daiyamōdo ni me ga kurami* ('Blinded by Dia-Mode', Toray Dia-Mode), a play on *daiyamondo ni me ga kurami* ('Blinded by diamonds') from Ozaki Kōyō's novel *Konjiki Yasha (The Gold Demon)*; Sharp's *Shin channeru jijō* ('New channel conditions'), which takes off Fukuzawa Yukichi's *Seiyō Jijō (Western Conditions)* and Fukada Yusuke's *Shin Seiyō Jijō (New Western Conditions)*; and Maipi's *Chichi kaeru* ('Father changes'), which uses the title of a Kikuchi Kan drama, but puns on the fact that *kaeru* can mean 'change' (nappies), as well as 'return' (home).

Another advertisement, for Diana boots, makes use of Shakespeare's *Taming of the Shrew* as its slogan (*Jaja uma narashi*), and the great bard gets a second hearing back home in the *Sunday Express*'s *2p or not 2p. Nigel's budget by Nigel.* In general, though, it would seem as if English advertisers prefer not to go too far back in time when it comes to sounding off the theatre. That *A Man For All Seasons*, by Robert Bolt, is their clear favourite can be seen in:

> *A can for all seasons* (Lyle's Golden Syrup)
> *A card for all reasons* (Visa Premier Card)

Music, in one form or another, and personalities connected with the world of popular music are frequently alluded to in advertising. For example:

> *Porky and Best* (Wall's Sausages)
> *Fairy tales can come true* (Martini)
> *C'mon Colman's, light my fire* (Colman's)[5]
> *Goodness gracious, great ball of cheese!* (Edam)
> *Goodbye Piccadilly, farewell Leicester Square* (G.L.C.)
> *The way down yonder to New Orleans* (American Airlines)
> *Got a brand new way to Denver, John* (American Airlines)

Japanese advertisements pun on their indigenous popular songs, frequently crooned in *karaoke* bars. *Tokyo Night Club*, by Frank Nagai and Matsuo Kazuko, was turned into *Tōkyō natto kurabu* ('Tokyo *natto* bean curd club') by Hakutsuru when it advertised its '*sake* pack', and Kobayashi Akira's *Mukashi no namae de dete imasu* ('Appearing in its old name') was used by Isetan Department Store to point out that during its bargain sale goods were being sold at their old prices (*Mukashi no nedan de dete imasu*). Occasionally, advertisers play with Western songs—as with Toshiba's television commercial for a word processor in which various *kanji* characters, all reading *yu*, are backed by a Duke Aces melody *You, You, You.*

It is clear that there is a lot of linguistic cross-referencing between different areas of each society's culture. *Power to the people* (Ever Ready) alludes not just to John Lennon's song of the same title (1971) but to the slogan of the Black Panther movement

(1969), while *Sports fans of the world, unite!* (N.E.C.) harks back to the *Communist Manifesto*. *French Connection* is both book, film and fashion boutique. Advertising has come to form a vast mosaic (McLuhan 1964: 202) with the media, as television comedians, script writers, newspaper journalists and editors all jostle with one another to make use of verbal images.

How else is one to interpret Ruddles's *What every beer wants to be when it grows up*—unless as a play on the bumper sticker of a Mini, *I want to be a Rolls Royce, when I grow up? 'Aspara de ikinukō. Faito de ikō. Ribobitan D'*, writes Yamaguchi Hitomi, taking off a famous slogan for an energy drink in his novel, *Eburimanshi no yūga na seikatsu. Compulsive phewing* asserts an ad for a finance magazine (Market Eye); *nyūsu kaisetsu* ('New vinegar explanation') puns an ad by Mitsukan, playing on the title of a television programme ('News explanation'). *All disquiet on the Southern front* reads a newspaper headline in Britain; *Discover Japan* reads another that adopts a famous Japan National Railways campaign slogan. In other words, the 'total communication' effect of advertising (achieved through photography, type sizes, slogans, visual and verbal strategies) has been carried over into a large number of newspapers and magazines. As Raymond Williams has pointed out, 'a style of communication developed for the selling of products, has to a considerable extent taken over the presentation of news and opinion' (1976: 101). In the media mosaic, everyone is sounding off everyone else. McLuhan's dictum that the medium is the message may not be true (Eco 1986: 235), but there can be no doubt that the message is often no more—and no less—than the media.

Notes

1 Most of the Japanese examples cited in this section are taken from Yasuda 1984, and Yasuda & Ya: uda 1985.

2 More remarkable are slogans like *Kotoshi mottomo chūmoku sarete iru shingatasha 626* (Mazda) which appeared in a combination of *kanji* characters and *hiragana* syllabary, but was accompanied by a bracketed free translation: ('The all New 626, Japan's Car of the Year'). At one stage, I thought that Mazda's decision to put out a slogan which could not be read by almost the entire population of the United Kingdom had something to do with the current fad

amongst young people for wearing T shirts and blouses with Chinese characters printed on them. This view, I now realise, is a little simplistic. Rather, the pervasive use in British advertising of Japanese writing and images (which go back to the end of the nineteenth century) is almost certainly part of a more general process of 'Orientalism' criticised by Said (1979).

3 There was a period during the mid 1980s when the media got excited over Britain's then 'most eligible bachelor'. A television commercial for Carlsberg had two frogs discussing a prince's budding romance with a girl, while the following extract purports to have been written by one potential fiancee, Ms Tracie Lamb, to her mother and describes Prince Andrew: 'He told us his greatest fantasy was to go to a party dressed as a frog, kiss the prettiest girl and tell her he was a prince' (*Time*, 18 April 1983).

4 Yukijirushi, Snow Brand, cheese is responsible for the following '*haiku*': *yu agari ni / bīru to chīzu / iu koto naski* ('After a bath, beer and cheese. Nothing [more] to be said').

5 One advertisment in the Colman's series depicts a Japanese *o-iran* (courtesan) in the process of being enwrapped by a fire breathing dragon.

9

The sounds of cultural discourse

Introduction

It is clear that there is a continual two-way process by which the language of advertising infiltrates the language of communication as a whole. In this way, advertising slogans help form the structures of meaning by which modern industrialised societies are organised.

This is, of course, the real 'art' of advertising: to translate between systems of meaning and to create 'a vast meta-system where values from different areas of our lives are made interchangeable' (Williamson 1978: 25). That advertising has been successful in this respect can be seen, for example, in the way that we have come to regard as more or less 'normal' the link between cars and cosmetics, as in: *Race bred for the fast lane* (Rover); and *Life in the fast lane* (Turbo After Shave).

It may well be that, like the Japanese, we ourselves will in due course automatically equate the idea of travel with food, if slogans of the following kind continue to haunt our billboards:

Feast on a great American special
Roast in the Med this summer from £145
Mix with fresh greens this summer from £99 (All Thomas Cook)
Summer is now being served (Greek National Tourist Organisation)

So how is this discourse created? English advertisements commonly create continuity between advertiser and product. John Player, for example, has produced a whole series of slogans based on its black-packaged cigarettes:

Tail Black   *Play it Black*
Black Chat   *Black and front*
Black Stage   *Black on the Rails*
Black on Broadway

and so on, often placed strategically by roads, theatres, or railway stations. Alternatively, they can be topical, as with the Christmas 1983 slogan: *Black on the cards*. Similarly, American Airlines has created the following series of slogans, based on the network of cities to which the company flies:

Dallas without the dilly dally
Phoenix phast
San Antonio, sans delay
Seattle without the hassle, and
How to appear nightly in Las Vegas

The examples quoted here may be termed as 'immediate', in that the advertiser concerned put out the slogans one after another over a continuous period of time. Other series, such as:

Guinness is good for you, and
Guinless isn't good for you

are less immediate and involve a time lag of some decades. The same is true of Rowntree's recent introduction of a number of variations on its old advertisement for fruit gums, current between 1958 and 1961:

Don't forget the fruit gums, mum, with
Don't forget
Mums remember
Dads shouldn't forget, either
Grandmas remember, too

Advertising sounds

Now, it seems to me that the discourse techniques of English advertising are in fact rather similar to a form of ritual insult found in Black communities in the United States and known generically as *sounding*, or referred to by such other terms as *woofing* in Philadelphia, *joning* in Washington, and *signifying* in Chicago.

Whatever its name locally, sounding usually follows a similar pattern, as in this series of sounds quoted by Labov (1972: 311):

133

Your mother got on sneakers!
Your mother wear high-heeled sneakers in church!
Your mother wear a jock strap.
Your mother got polka-dot drawers!
Your mother wear the seat of her drawers on the top of her head!

As can be seen here, sounds are partly repetitive and partly creative, frequently substituting certain words while retaining the same syntactic form. What happens is that one member of a group of men sounds on a comment made by another, who then retaliates by transforming the original sound. A third person has to be present for the sounding to take on meaning as verbal sparring, and he may himself participate in the game at an opportune moment (Goffman, quoted in Labov 1972: 343–4).

A: *Your mother eat coke-a-roaches.*
B: *Your mother eat fried dick-heads.*
A: *Your mother suck fried dick-heads.*
C: *His mother eat* cold *dick-heads.* (p. 348)

There is an obvious parallel between this kind of exchange and what happened, for example, in the case of the Esso slogan: *Put a tiger in your tank*, which gave rise to a number of derivatives, including:

Put a tiger in your tummy (Anonymous hamburger stand)
Put a tiger in your tankard (Tiger Beer)
Put a tankard in your tiger (Standard Rochester Beer)

Similarly, a 1962 Peanuts book by Charles Schulz, titled *Happiness is a Warm Puppy*, has been responsible for numerous sounds in English advertising:

Happiness is egg-shaped (Egg Marketing Board)
Happiness is a quick-starting car (Esso)
Happiness is a cigar called Hamlet

Other examples include the Lennon and McCartney song *Happiness is a warm gun*, and the more recent *Nappiness is baby-shaped* (Peau-douce).

There are numerous examples of this sort of linguistic borrowing which frequently takes the form of parody discussed earlier. Hence, we have the questionable:

I'm Margie. Fly me (National Airlines)
I'm meaty. Fry me (Wall's Sausages)

or the long-running slogan for Turkish Delight chocolate: *Full of Eastern promise*, which suddenly emerged in the early 1980s as:

Turkey's delight (Colman's Mustard)
Full of East End promise (John Bull)

with the latter punning on the fact that the manufacturer of the beer in question, Romford Brewery, is located in the east end of London.

In fact, beer brewers appear to be among the more fervent participants in slogan adoption and adaptation. Carlsberg, for instance, has created a series of slogans which has played on the fact that its lager is made in Denmark and drunk in (among other places) Britain:

The Danish can. The British do
Born in Denmark. Raised in Britain
In Denmark it reigns. In Britain it pours

The last of these slogans is based on an earlier advertisement put out by Guinness in 1977 during the Jubilee celebrations marking the 25th anniversary of the Queen of England's coronation: *We've poured through the Reign.*

Another extensive series of advertising sounds has developed from Heineken's *Heineken refreshes the parts that other beers cannot reach*, which has attracted attention because the slogan has been linked with amusing visuals involving the revival of policemen's toes after long hours on the beat, or Concorde's drop snoot which straightens up after being refuelled with Heineken. The obvious success of the original slogan has led to:

Renault reaches the parts other cars cannot reach
It seems to be refreshing parts that even I cannot reach (William Younger)
If you drink too much there's one part that every beer can reach (Health Education Council)

but Heineken has returned to the fray by giving its original slogan a number of neat twists, such as:

Heineken refreshes the parched other beers cannot reach
Heineken refreshes the pirates other beers cannot reach
Heineken refreshes the parrots other beers cannot reach
Heineken refreshes the pets other beers cannot reach

and of Les Patterson, the slobbering Australian politician created by the comic, Barry Humphreys: *Beyond reach.*

As Labov points out, sounding in American Black communities tends to pick on a *ritualised*, rather than real, attribute of a person. The whole notion of sounding, indeed, rests on the fact that it is based on palpable untruths, and this is why it is classified as a form of ritual insult. Similarly, in the context of advertising, it seems that the more unlikely the message of the slogan, the more likely it will become the object of sounding. There is, after all, no evidence to show that Heineken actually can refresh the parts other beers cannot reach; nor is it literally possible to put a tiger in a car petrol tank.

At the same time, sounding in advertising differs from that found in Black communities precisely because slogans are not ritual *insults*. Rivals do not insult each other in order to 'win' the game of sounds. They merely try to create a successful slogan which will catch the public's imagination. When an 'insult' does occur, as, for example, in Volvo's *Bodyguards cost less than escorts*, it is personal (against Ford), rather than ritual, in form and is unlikely to occur as part of the general practice of sounding.

Abrahams (1974: 246) has distinguished between three types of street talk: *information, manipulation* and *play*. Between the first and the last can be found a general shift from content to form. With sounding *per se*, it is not the message itself that is important so much as the artful form of the utterance. It would seems that advertising slogans follow a similar pattern:

informative: *Triple crown victor in Paris-Daker rally* (Mitsubishi Pajero)

manipulative: *Shapes you as Nature intended* (Naturama bra)

play: *Cool, calm and collect it* (Guinness)

It is when a slogan is manipulative and involves play that it is likely to become the object of sounding by other advertisers.

Precisely because of the play involved in sounding, we find that among young Black Americans laughter is the main sign of approval. A man's reputation is made by his ability to sound and sound successfuly, putting his rivals down. His talent is immediately recognised and appraised by other members of his group. Similarly, advertising slogans are quickly evaluated by members of the public whom they address and successful ones are talked about. The difference here is that advertisers are not immediately aware of the effect of their slogans, since they stand outside the group of people whom they address.

Although advertisers cannot interact with groups of people in the way that Black Americans do when sounding, it is clear that they do encourage the formation of in-group cliques of consumers attracted to certain products. Williams (1976: 102–3) has commented on the way in which advertisers seek to establish 'types' through such forms of social classification as:

The Martini set
Top people take The Times
The Pepsi Generation
Join the Professionals (British Army Recruitment)

What is of interest in this context is that when sounding on slogans occurs, it frequently does so among companies advertising similar products. This is not always the case (as the varitions on the *Happiness is ...* theme reveal), but advertising—particularly in its use of puns—incites to complicity and 'clubability' (Redfern 1982: 275). To the extent that consumer in-groupism is encouraged by sounding in advertising, it plays a similar role to that played by sounding in American Black communities.

The major social classification reflected in advertising is that between men and women, and sexism in slogans (and visuals) understandably arouses the ire of women (feminists or not):

Isn't it time you flirted with your wife? Other men do
Forget that she's your wife, remember she's a woman (both De Beers)

Less heavy-handed allusions to sex include:

Man and high performance machine in perfect harmony (Ford)
It looks even better on a man (Tootal)

Often sounding in Black communities involves insults of a sexual nature, particularly against the opponent's mother, and this has been seen as a consequence of the matrifocal family in which boys are brought up (Hannerz 1969: 134). While it would be absurd to draw a parallel conclusion about sounding in advertising, there are two points which deserve further consideration. First, why are slogans seen to be sexist? Second, why it is that, when advertising sounding does occur, it seems to be confined to those commodities specifically connected in people's minds with 'masculinity' and 'sexuality'—alcohol, cars, fashion, jewellery and cosmetics? These questions suggest a further analogy between sounding in American Black communities and in advertising. In both instances, the verbal play is basically addressed to *men*.

Japan's cultural discourse

This has been a somewhat lengthy diversion away from Japan ('thank Buddha!', some may exclaim), as I have tried to show a second aspect of the 'poetic' function of British advertising language. The obvious question that arises from my analogy of sounding is, what of Japanese advertising slogans? Do they go in for the same kind of bantering humour? Do they take one another off?

The answer is that of course they do, but in a manner somewhat different from English advertisements. We have already come across examples of Japanese slogans that play on other aspects of the media, so that in this respect they can be said to 'sound'. Advertisers will also make use of a single slogan structure, with word variations, as in one of Parco's campaigns:

fasshon datte, mane dake ja dame da
Fashion is not just imitation

moderu datte, kao dake ja dame da
A model is not just a pretty face

Alternatively, they will use the same slogan with different visuals, as in Shiseidō's *hikatteru ne, ano ko* ('Sparkling, isn't she?').

In general, however, they do not seem to play with *grammatical structures* in the way that English advertising does. Perhaps this is not surprising, given the conclusions of the previous chapter. Moreover, I have already argued that the language of modernity in Japan tends to focus on certain keywords—specifically, that advertising supports an 'internal cultural debate' on the respective roles of group, individual and *seishin* in contemporary Japanese society.

But there is, I think, another way in which 'sounding' occurs as other discourses are initiated, or taken up, by advertisers. In the early 1980s, for example, there was a sudden flurry of television commercials and magazine advertisements that made much of the English word 'city'. Honda appears to have started the craze when it produced its new mini car, the Honda *City*, and used the British pop group Madness to provide the backing song (*In the city*). A magazine slogan for the same product ran: *shitī wa, nyūsu ni afureteru* ('The City is bursting with news'), and this was taken up by a new range of saucepans put out by National and called *Metal City*. At the same time, the English word was translated into Japanese:

> *Tokai no hito no shizensui* (Suntory mineral water)
> *City people's natural water*
>
> *Tokaijin yo!* (Kagome vegetable juice)[1]
> *Urbanites!*

In this way, advertisers brought out into the open a second debate that has hovered in the background of Japan's economic development (if not of contemporary British society): the discrepancy in ideals between those living in the countryside and those inhabiting urban areas. Given that these ideals tend to centre on 'traditional' and 'modern' Japan respectively, the discourse in fact takes up the 'group' and 'individual' debate discussed earlier, though rephrasing it in slightly different terms.

Another ideal that has had a good run for its money in the mid-1980s is that of 'intelligence', which has appeared in at least three different forms: *chisei* ('intelligence'), *chiteki* ('intelligent'), and the English *interijensu* (sometimes written in the Roman alphabet as 'intelligence', although somewhat different from the English in nuance). Tanaka (1989) has shown that this ideal is used in advertisements that address themselves to women in particular. For example:

> *chiteki de jōhin na shiruku burausu* (Tokyo Blouse)
> An intelligent and noble silk blouse
>
> *chisei to yasei, San Rōran no ganchiku* (Yves Saint Laurent)
> Intelligence and wildness—Saint Laurent's suggestion
>
> *kono aki no shuryū wa, yahari chiteki de sekushii* (Robe)
> The main trend this autumn, as you may have guessed, is to be intelligent and sexy
>
> *egao mo onna no chisei ka shira* (Narisu Cosmetics)
> Is it that a smiling face is also a woman's intelligence?

Intelligence.
Sore ga kimi no utsukushisa.
Kite iru fuku ni chisei o kanjiru.
Tatta ippon no kuchibeni kara mo ... (Kanebo)

Intelligence.
That is [the secret of] your beauty.
Your intelligence is seen in the clothes that you wear.
Even in the single lipstick [that you put on].[2]

However, just as I have suggested that words like *kosei* do not really reflect 'individuality' in contemporary Japanese society, so Tanaka argues that advertising slogans like these, although seeming to make a distinction between male and female 'intelligence' and to praise women for being 'intelligent', in fact define such intelligence as part of the typical female role model of 'good wife and wise mother' (*ryōsai kenbo*). In other words, while pretending to speak the language of modernity, advertisers are doing their best to keep women firmly in their place. In this respect, it would seem that Japanese and English advertisers share a common attitude.

I think it possible to go a little further here. One common insult (common to both English and Japanese alike) hurled by those living in urban areas is that of the 'country bumpkin' or *inakappei*. Secure in the belief that cities act as the repositories of Culture (with a capital C), urbanites have been convinced that country people are 'ignorant'. This, of course, is the 'under meaning' (*ura imi*) of Yanagi's praise for the simple country craftsman, who had to be 'unlearned' (*mugaku*) and at 'one with nature' in order to create beauty for what was, after all, a group of city aesthetes. I have already pointed out the extent to which folk-craft theory was very much a product of its time—a time when Japan was going through a stage of rapid urbanisation. Although this process received a temporary setback during and immediately after the Pacific War, Japan's cities have continued to expand and to soak up the rural population. It would seem, then, that by using 'intelligence' as a keyword in their slogans, advertisers are not only commenting upon the role of women but are also participating in the on-going discourse between country and city, in contemporary Japanese society.

Conclusion

I suppose that in conclusion we ought to ask how seriously the metaphor in the phrase *cultural discourse* ought to be taken. In England, it is certainly the case that we can participate actively in the verbal play of advertisements and create our own sounds. The following series, for example, owes less to the ingenuity of the advertisers than to the fact that I happened to see each slogan while going up or down the escalators of London's Underground stations:

> *The way down yonder to New Orleans* (American Airlines)
> *When Prohibition hit Southern Comfort, New Orleans discovered the Blues*
> *It hasn't gone underground since prohibition* (Jim Bean)
> *Ideas above your station* (Tatler)

In this respect, English advertising seems to offer the individual more 'freedom of choice' than do Japanese slogans which focus on the same linguistic images time and time again. Again, in England we may try to answer advertisements back by writing our own graffiti on them—something that I have yet to see in the Japanese environment of strict law and order:

> *To Volvo a son. 4,397 pounds*
> Better luck next time
> *The Pils to be taken seriously* (Lowenbrau)
> Kill men
> *New. Mild. And Marlboro*
> New. Vile. And a bore

together with the well-known

> *If it were a lady, it would get its bottom pinched* (Fiat 127)
> If this lady was a car, she'd run you down.[3]

All the same, in both England and Japan, advertising has an unpleasant habit of working 'in a circular movement which once set in motion is self-perpetuating' (Williamson 1978: 14). The Guinless slogan is a good example of the way advertisers adapt to criticism in this manner (the criticism that alcohol can be 'good' for people). So, however much creativity there is in graffiti abuse, it does not act to change the *status quo* all the time (Parkin 1980:

62). Advertisers always end up dictating the course along which they wish their 'discourse' to proceed.

Perhaps, then, I have erred in giving this chapter the heading it now has, for even if we do accept the notion of discourse, there is certainly no question of its being a cultural 'dialogue', since it is a discourse without any built-in turn-taking system. In this respect, advertising language is more of a 'rhetoric' (Redfern 1982: 272) which, like political oratory (Bloch 1975), serves to stifle debate. Advertising agencies clearly do not design their slogans in anticipation of what the public might say in reply. Consequently, the individual is reduced to adopting the only communicative role which such a situation leaves open: that of cultural heckler.

Notes

1 This slogan in itself may have prompted Lowenbrau's *bīrujin yo!* ('Beer-ites!').
2 All the above examples are taken from Tanaka 1989.
3 All taken from Posener 1982.

10

The good, the bad
and the noodle western

Introduction

To be a cultural heckler in Japan is not easy. Things may well change, of course, but hitherto the rhetoric of popular culture has tended to keep the Japanese firmly in their social place. It is true that there are certain cultural forms—like some types of the *manga* comics, for example—that threaten to take apart the tight web of morality in which post-war society has been woven, but there is a tendency for them all to be sucked by the capitalist spider into its (post-) industrial labyrinth and made central to it.[1] Thus comics become no more than 'an effective and often polite way of transmitting information' (Schodt 1983: 148) in a society that, even more than our own under a similarly conservative regime, places great emphasis on the value of information in an attempt to prevent questioning and real debate.

That the Japanese have been prepared to accept all this may well have something to do with their Confucian background. Dore (1965) has traced in some detail the continuity between 'feudal' Tokugawa and 'modern' Meiji Japan, and shown how the values of harmony, co-operation and obligation inherent in the Neo-Confucian classics were adopted by the newly emerging national regime. Even today, it would seem to be in terms of Confucian—rather than Shinto or Buddhist—ideals that we should consider people's interpretations of morality in modern Japanese society. Thus, in the following analysis of *jidaigeki* 'noodle westerns', I shall argue that the essentially Confucian relationships depicted in the dramas not only focus on the ambivalent relationship between group and individual in Japanese society; they also enter into a wider cultural debate on the relative importance of tradition and modernisation, of oriental 'spiritualism' *vis-à-vis* western 'materialism'. I suspect, moreover, that the Confucian cultural debate within Japan is carried over into anthropologists' interpretations of the way in which Japanese society is organised. In other words, we have 'good' theories and 'bad' theories, depending on which side of the group/individual irrigation ditch we prefer to squat.

Confucianism, principle and ether

Although we use the term 'Confucianism' in English after the name of Confucius—the man who is popularly believed to have taught the doctrine—we might perhaps start by noting that the Chinese term is *ju chiao* (*jukyō* in Japanese) and strictly means 'the doctrine of the literati'. It is, therefore, perhaps incorrect to call Confucianism a 'religion' as such, since its concerns are essentially secular and centre on rules of conduct according to social proprieties and political principles. Weber has written that: 'In the absence of all metaphysics and almost all residues of religious anchorage, Confucianism is rationalist to such a fargoing extent that it stands at the extreme boundary of what one might possibly call a 'religious' ethic. At the same time, Confucianism is more rationalist and sober, in the sense of the absence and the rejection of all non-utilitarian yardsticks, than any other ethical system, with the possible exception of J. Bentham's' (Weber 1947: 293). Although Weber's version of Confucianism is in certain respects idealised (as we shall soon learn to our cost when we discuss neo-Confucian metaphysics), in general it can be said perhaps that Confucianism is an ethico-political system which has shaped Chinese civilisation for more than two millenia, and which has been alive and well—although occasionally slipping into uncharacteristic disguises—in Japan for the past 1,500 years. In particular, perhaps, it should have suffered from its latest escapade when—like the wolf in the *Tale of Little Red Riding Hood*—Confucianism decided to hop into Grandma Shinto's bed. From there it leaped with pearly teeth, harbouring bombastic designs upon us children of the Occident, who were saved only by the tenacity of a gum-chewing lumberjack. The question is: did Confucianism die with the wolf? Or did it manage to escape into another, less provocative disguise?

Confucianism's main focus of attention has been its social philosophy that man should live in harmony with the laws of heaven by maintaining what are known as the Five Fundamental Relationships (*wu ch'ang*, or *gojō* in Japanese): between ruler and minister, father and son, husband and wife, elder brother and younger brother, and friend and friend. These relationships are accompanied by certain duties and obligations. The ruler should be righteous and his minister loyal; the father affectionate and his son filial; a husband harmonious and his wife submissive; an elder brother friendly and his younger brother respectful; and friends mutually sincere. These are the keywords of Confucian thought, and to them are added the four (occasionally five) virtues of benevolence, righteousness, wisdom, decorum (and sincerity). Hence, Confucianism espouses a moral doctrine that is primarily concerned with the ordering of the state by government. Men of superior qualities at the top of the social hierarchy are supposed to set a good example and so influence the popular masses under their control. Men have distinct roles which they should perform for the sake of society, and society itself is arranged in an orderly manner. If those in charge of government apply the moral principles inherent in the four virtues, social harmony will ensue. Morality is instilled in others by virtue rather than by force.

Alas! L. R. Mauré's Law of Opposition does not apply here, for Confucianism is not as unconfused as the last paragraph might lead us to believe. During the Sung Dynasty (960–1279), Confucianism in China underwent fairly radical re-interpretation as philosophers tried to answer some of the intellectual problems raised by Buddhist thought. While Buddhism emphasised transience and impermanence, Confucianism insisted on the reality of the self and of the universe. If a black hole existed, it was not in space (the Buddhist void), but in Calcutta (Confucian reality). Somehow the two modes of thought had to be reconciled, and it was this realisation that forced Chinese intellectuals in the Sung period to think Confucian ethics into metaphysics. Western philosophers will no doubt be as sceptical of their methods as physicists are of professional spoon-benders, but I shall proceed because neo-Confucian explanations of the universe happen to coincide with my interpretation of the workings of Japanese social organisation.

Neo-Confucianism is the title given to what was essentially a synthesis of Buddhist, Taoist and Confucian ideas.[2] The most famous of the neo-Confucian scholars was Chu Hsi (1130–1200) who, adopting some of the ideas of his predecessors, distinguished between metaphysical 'above shapes' (*keijijō* in Japanese) and physical, concrete 'below shapes' (*keijika*). What existed above shapes had, as its name implied, neither shape nor form; it transcended both time and space. This Chu Hsi called *li* (*ri* in Japanese), or 'immaterial principle'. What existed below shapes he called *ch'i* (*ki*), 'material force' or 'ether'. *Ch'i* lay within the bounds of space and time, and so had actuality and form.

Chu Hsi argued that *li* had no creative power of its own and had to rely on the transformations of *yin* (quiescence) and *yang* (movement) within *ch'i* to give it form. Yet, at the same time, *li* had *a priori* existence over *ch'i*. Chu Hsi's duality of immaterial principle and material force thus strike me as being somewhat similar to de Saussure's distinction between *langue* and *parole*. Both *langue* and *li* can exist in an ideal vacuum, but they rely upon *parole* and *ch'i* to give them substantial form.[3] This is what might be called a 'Blue Flame' theory: the genie may be hovering somewhere around, but he is not allowed to make an official appearance until Aladdin rubs his lamp.

Li is a supremely good, normative principle—equivalent, at the metaphysical level, to Aristotle's Prime Mover and, at the level of moral values, to Plato's Idea of the Good. *Ch'i*, however, would appear to be potentially imperfect; for when it combines with *li* to form things and people, it produces clever people and dull people, kind people and cruel people, and so on. This suggests that *li* can lose perfection when it is activated by *ch'i*—in much the same way as we can imagine a perfectly round circle, but tend to end up drawing a somewhat elliptical wobble.

Nevertheless, Chu Hsi argued that man's essential nature was good, and so adopted Mencius's position rather than that of Hsun-tzu, who said that human nature was evil, or that of Han Yu, who suggested that there were three kinds of human nature—good, bad and a mixture of both. For Chu Hsi, human nature had to be good because principle was good and human nature was principle. Where there was imperfection, this was in man's *physical* nature as a result of *ch'i*.

The distinction between essential and physical nature coincides with that between *li* and *ch'i* and gives rise to certain moral values. Man's sense of filial duty, loyalty, honesty and so on (attributes connected with the Five Fundamental Relationships), together with his understanding of the Four Virtues, all came from his endowment of *li*. However, his physical nature produced feelings, and feelings in themselves gave rise to selfish desires (*yü*, or *yoku* in Japanese). It would thus appear that an excess, or insufficiency of, desire is responsible for evil, since it leads man away from the perfection of principle which is in his essential nature.

The relation between *li*, principle, and *ch'i*, ether, has been the subject of considerable debate on both sides of the China Sea, for neo-Confucianism was to some extent adopted by the Japanese when Tokugawa Ieyasu (1542–1616) set about unifying the country at the beginning of the seventeenth century. From then on, two types of neo-Confucian thought have existed, one stressing principle (*ri* in Japanese) and the other ether (*ki*) (de Bary 1979: 19).

I do not wish to dwell too long on historical facts, but it might be pointed out here that each of the major thinkers of the Tokugawa period (1603–1868) was concerned with human nature and its inherent goodness or evil. Fujiwara Seika (1561–1619) saw emotions as the source of selfish desires and hence potentially evil. Hayashi Razan (1583–1657) felt that physical nature was not necessarily evil and that principle could hardly exist unless embodied in ether. Yamaga Sokō (1622–85) followed Mencius in thinking that man was by nature good. If selfish desires were bad, then it implied that the actual self was also evil; so Sokō proceeded to distinguish between desire permitted by heaven (public desire) and desire that was merely personal (private desire). Itō Jinsai (1627–1705) tried to separate man's essential nature from principle, for he felt that Sung Dynasty neo-Confucianism had allowed the individual too much self-expression and not enough restraint. Spontaneity, in Jinsai's opinion, could destroy social morality if it were too subjective. Finally, Ogyū Sorai (1666–1728) agreed with Jinsai, but felt that human nature could be perfected only by becoming involved in society, rather than by cultivating an inner moral growth, as Jinsai had suggested (de Bary 1979: 127–86). Is all this an idle con, a fusion of ideas, or plain confusion?

Behind each of these slight shifts in neo-Confucian thought in

Japan seems to lie one basic concern: to what extent is the individual bound by Confucian ethical principles, or duties, known as *giri* ('socially contracted dependence'), and how much can be allow his spontaneity, *ninjō* ('human feelings'), to affect his social relations? In other words, as principle (*ri*) is to ether (*ki*), so is society to the individual and *giri* to *ninjō*. What is more, this dialogue between *giri* and *ninjō* (which is, after all, merely the social application of the dialogue between the metaphysical principle and the physical ether) still goes on and is to be found at the heart of Japan's internal cultural debate.

It is perhaps surprising to find that Confucian ethics have survived the lumberjack's felling of Grandma Shinto at the end of the not so Pacific War. After all, at one stage Confucian ideals were looked upon with some scepticism, and the widely propagated and accepted statements of Confucian-cum-Shinto ideology that sustained Japan's military nationalism before the war came to be seen as part of a 'feudal' past which could scarcely contemplate courtship with the postwar bride of Western industrial capitalism. I would suggest, however, that Confucian ideals are still important in modern Japanese society and that they form part of the country's internal cultural debate over such problems as the relationship between tradition and modernisation, between an 'oriental spiritual civilisation' and a 'Western materialist civilisation', between society and individual and—ultimately—between concepts of good and evil. In order to illustrate this argument, I want to take a look at what I shall here refer to as the 'noodle western' (or 'spaghetti eastern', depending on one's culinary and geographical tastes).

Confucian ethics and the noodle western

The television genre known as *jidaigeki*, to which I have irreverently referred as the 'noodle western', consists of films about *samurai. Jidaigeki* literally means 'period drama' and refers to any film whose story takes place prior to the Meiji Restoration of 1868. Films can be full-length features for cinema, as with Kurosawa Akira's *Kage musba* or Kobayashi Masaki's *Hara-kiri*, but here I will be talking about the somewhat less intense and more frivolous television films shown almost nightly on one of Japan's many television channels. These films are generally about fifty minutes long and centre on Robin-Hood-type heroes who perform miraculous deeds for the benefit of society. In both content and methods of direction, the *jidaigeki* are comparable to the spaghetti western, and a number of American films have either copied, or been parodied by, their Japanese counterparts. *The Magnificent Seven*, for example, is a straight copy of *Shichinin no samurai* (*The Seven Samurai*); the *Sanbiki no samurai* parodies the western gunfight that concludes *The Good, the Bad and the Ugly*.

In the noodle western television films, what might be termed the 'semiotics' of good and evil are made abundantly clear, and are similar to what we have come to expect of spaghetti westerns. Thunder, lightning and heavy rain, for example, signify danger (and rain, occasionally, acts as a metaphor for the tears of despair). A night-watchman patrolling the streets and clapping his wooden sticks rhythmically, as he calls out dolefully 'Take care of fires!' (*hi no yōjin*), almost invariably signifies the peaceful prelude to action—a swordfight or, more probably, a robbery. If it is a moonlit night, it is more than likely that the break-in will be conducted by magical *ninja* spies, who can do standing jumps ten feet into the air, run soundlessly across tiled rooftops and hurl sharp metal stars with the accuracy of expert dart players. A man eating buckwheat noodles at a noodle vendor's store is a 'goody', as is the kimonoed girl with flower in her hair and leaning very slightly to one side as she trips along in her wooden clogs—like a reed bending in the breeze. At the same time, her very fragility is a premonition of her luckless fate. The unkempt *rōnin sumurai*, with *sake* bottle slung from hip or over his shoulder, tends to be cast as the 'baddy'—as is the bald priest, the merchant or the lord who is filmed consulting his cronies with a candle's flame flickering in front of his face.[4]

These oppositions of day and night, light and dark, clean and dirty all support the basic contrast of good and bad. Heroes are well washed, clean-looking, closely shaven. They wear well-barbered wigs and well cut kimonos with bright and tasteful designs. They emanate purity. Villains, for their part, have oily skins and sweat freely. They dress in dark robes of cotton or luxurious silk, depending on their social status, and have menacing—so obviously evil—laughs. They are neither polite nor humble like the heroes, but rough and rude, and occasionally obsequious. It is as easy for the viewer to feel immediate revulsion for the bad as it is for him or her to identify with the good. The system of signs used in *jidaigeki* demands very little in the way of *parole*-like interpretation.

The plots of noodle westerns are similarly simple and demand little intellectual concentration. A young girl is murdered for accidentally witnessing a robbery; a hardworking young apprentice is tricked into betraying his master; a crooked policeman is bribed by a merchant or feudal lord to overlook certain irregularities. In every case revenge is taken by a heroic *samurai*, an honest policeman or down-to-earth citizens turned magically, like Cinderella's mice, into merry men in the service of a Tokugawa-period Robin Hood. Every film starts with society being disordered in some way or other—by murder, robbery or other forms of violence. Every film ends with a return to normality. Like ritual, it conjoins two initially separate people or groups of people (both or all of whom end up on the side of the good) (*cf.* Lévi-Strauss 1966: 32).

But what, you may ask, has all this got to do with Confucianism? Earlier on, I mentioned such concepts as the Five Fundamental Relationships and the Four Virtues, by which Confucian scholars have argued that society should be organised. These social relationships and moral virtues are an essential part of the noodle western. They form the very moral foundation upon which characters are expected to build their social contacts. It is according to whether they do or do not behave according to the Four Virtues, do or do not respect the Five Fundamental Relationships, that they are distinguished as 'good' or 'bad'.

It is our old friend 'principle' (*ri*) that underlies almost all action in the *jidaigeki*, for it is according to principle that social laws are seen to be natural laws. You have only to behave according to these natural laws of socially contracted dependence, or *giri*— which is defined by the virtues of humaneness, righteousness, wisdom and decorum—and you know precisely how society will react towards you. If you behave well and follow *giri*, society will treat you well and all will turn out well. If you disregard these laws, however, you will be treated unfavourably by others and will in the end get your just desserts. Good will *always* prevail; evil will *always* be defeated. If one of the goodies does get killed, he or she will be avenged by others. Whatever a baddy's status in society, he will be caught and punished.[5] Thus society, as depicted in the *jidaigeki*, is a well-knit organism which invariably rectifies its faults. By follwing principle, people can become perfect social beings.

If *everybody* followed principle, of course, there would be no baddies in the noodle westerns. This is where ether (*ki*) comes in, in the form of human feelings (*ninjō*). Provided that *ninjō* remains in accord with the Four Virtues, then it perfectly balances *giri* and suggests that each individual is a well-oiled cog in the harmonious wheels of Japanese society. But once somebody somewhere decides not to observe social decorum, humaneness or sincerity and allows his human feelings to follow the path of selfish desire, the cog wheels hiccup and grind to a halt.

And thereby hangs a tale. Just as Pooh and his friends persuaded an enlightened Owl to hand over his new bell rope so that it could be nailed back on to Eeyore's rump, so do characters in *jidaigeki* see the wisdom of the Five Fundamental Relationships.[6] In the small group that forms the basic entity in Japanese social organization, each member respects and is loyal to other members. People help one another as friends; and yet, at the same time, because the Japanese tend to frame their relations hierarchically, this friendship frequently takes the form of an elder brother–younger brother, or father–son, relationship. This can be seen with the two runners attached to the policeman, Zenigata Heiji; with Sukesan and Kakusan in the service of the disguised feudal lord, Mito Kōmon; or with the fire chief, Megumi no kashira, and his followers in *Abarembō Shōgun*.

There is a general emphasis in *jidaigeki* on kinship. A certain food will remind a heroine of her dead mother's cooking; a locket will remind a hero of his sister in childhood, and plots are filled with tales of lost sisters, of the search for a daughter, of the discovery of a missing brother, and so on. Women are compliant —unto death if needs be—and hence fulfil their fundamental social role of faithful mother, daughter, wife or sister.

These familial relationships are an important aspect of Confucian thought, which emphasises that a state can be well run only if people behave to strangers in the same way that they treat their nearest and dearest. It is perhaps not surprising, therefore, to find that in *jidaigeki* strangers are almost always taken into a family-type group and are given help and affection: the hungry are fed, the sick nursed back to health and the deprived taken into people's homes. And, in return, those who are helped are always prepared to repay what is seen to be social obligation.[7] No relationship between two people, once begun, by whatever stroke of chance, can ever end, except in death. Yet even by death the Japanese household is continued, and it is perhaps not surprising to find numerous scenes in *jidaigeki* of the goodies visiting graveyards. These are not quite such frightening, haunted places as they can be made to be in other types of film (both in Japan and in the West), but are places where people join together to respect the dead and look after their ancestors. It is the good who are buried; the evil dead are left to rot in the dust on which they fall.

The relationship between sovereign and people is another of the Five Fundamental Relationships given great importance in the noodle western. A number of film series has people from the highest echelons of society mingling with the masses. These characters are based on historical figures and include such eminent men as the 8th Shogun, Tokugawa Yoshimune (in *Abarembō Shōgun*), Ieyasu's grandson, Tokugawa Mitsukuni (in *Mito Komōn*), and nephew of the third Shogun Iemitsu, Matsudaira Chōshichirō (in *Tenka Gomen, Chōshichirō!*). Other characters, such as Momotaro Samurai, supposedly twin brother of one of the Tokugawa shoguns, may be based less on historical fact and more on a fanciful imagination which likes to suggest that sovereigns rule best when they fully understand the problems of their subjects.

These heroes lead double lives, infiltrating the lower levels of society and helping to keep order as they follow the Confucian precept of *kanzen chōaku*, encourage good and punish evil. Unrecognised, of course, by the simple townspeople with whom they consort, they prevent the spreading of corruption and the flouting of authority. They tangle with villains who come from the lowest stratum in the Tokugawa *shi-nō-kō-shō* four-class system (the merchants), and even from outside society altogether (*yakuza* gangsters and masterless *rōnin samurai*). But the very worst of the villains are those who, like the heroes themselves, come from the very top of society—feudal lords and senior *samurai* in government bureaucracy—and who make use of their elevated status to take advantage of innocent people and indulge in private profit, extravagance and luxury. They are assuredly evil, not only for their corruption and misuse of an authority entrusted to them by the shogun, but because they fail to lead lives of frugality espoused by Tokugawa Confucianism.

Dutifulness and loyalty remain the virtues that are practised by the good and that form the single path to redemption for the wayward villain. Obedience is demanded of people; even the baddies do as they are told, and the retainers of an evil lord will attack without question the *samurai* hero, even thought it is apparent that the hero just happens to be their overall lord and master! Immediate loyalties take precedence over more distant, and hence more impersonal, ones. These retainers never run away, even though thirty of them may have already been slashed to death by the hero's flailing sword. Cowardice is unmanly and contrary to the ethics of *bushidō*, or the way of the warrior. Death is an honour, especially at the hands of the high and mighty!

Another aspect of *jidaigeki* morality worth noting is honesty. Honesty always pays. In the end, someone will realise that the wronged goody is not telling lies, that he is in short a goody, and will come to his aid. Submissiveness and humility, too, are vital—particularly for women. The humble woman may be defiled (*watakushi no yō na kegareta onna*)—and note here how Shinto beliefs creep in to an essentially Confucian system—but her humility simultaneously makes her good, and we know that, in the end, she will be able to conquer the evil of her defilement and find an equally humble, 'harmonious' man to look after her.

Finally, trust is another major theme in the noodle western. 'Believe me' (*shinjite kure*) is a phrase used frequently by strangers, and even though there may not be any reason at this particular stage of the development of the plot for anyone to believe anyone else, characters are saved or damned by their capacity to trust the right or wrong person. Trust is thus ambiguous; it is good because it is close to sincerity (one of the Virtues when inflation increases them from four to five in number), but it can lead to suffering. All in all, however, society is seen to be safe and people find safety in social relations that are based on trusting one another.

Confucianism as cultural debate

Noodle westerns are not simply entertainment. Like all forms of entertainment, they contain within them certain social ideals. In particular, they advocate Confucius's notion of the five Fundamental Relationships and the Four Virtues. But why should people in present-day Japan be amenable to such ideals, given the disastrous consequences of Confucianism's alliance with Shinto nationalism in the 1930s? The answer to this question lies, I think, in Japan's response to westernisation and modern industrialisation. Just as in Tokugawa times Confucian ethics tried to deal with the role of the individual in Japanese society, so now they are used to combat what is seen to be the purely negative ideal of Western individualism. As we have seen in Chapter 4, Confucian ethics remain at the heart of a continuing dialogue about individual and group in Japanese social organisation.

First of all, it is clear that *jidaigeki* create a world that is purely Japanese. All films are set in an age when Japan was still isolated from Western influences. Moreover, they generally depict life during the Genroku era (1688–1704), a 'golden age' when—as in Tudor England—internal trade, the arts and other cultural activities flowered. It was during this era that the Tokugawa shoguns were at the zenith of their power and the *samurai* class was fully conscious and proud of *bushidō*, the way of the warrior (more of which in the next chapter). The country had been closed to foreigners for several decades (with the exception of a couple of trading posts in the south-western island of Kyushu), and the Japanese were discovering the glories of their own cultural achievements. Noodle westerns, then, depict a 'pure' Japan, untainted by the 'barbarism' of the 'red-haired devils' of the West. People wear kimonos and clothing with Japanese family crests. They have Japanese hairstyles. They eat Japanese food and drink Japanese *sake* or *shōchū*. They live in Japanese-style wooden houses, sleep in Japanese bedding laid out on *tatami* straw matting, and bathe in Japanese baths. They visit Japanese temples and speak a lauguage that is pure and uncontaminated by foreign words.

All of this presents an immediate contrast with present-day Japan, where people wear Western suits and dresses, have Western-style haircuts, frequently eat Western food and drink Western alcohol. They may now live in earthquake-proof concrete blocks of flats (generally referred to as 'mansions') and sleep in beds on wooden floors. Although they may still visit Japanese temples and shrines and bathe in Japanese-style baths, the modern Japanese will speak a language that frequently uses more English than Japanese vocabulary, so great is the number of foreign loan-words in vogue.

Second, while *jidaigeki* seek to remind modern Japanese that deep down they are 'different' from their Western counterparts in London, Paris or New York, they also point indirectly to problems that are seen to accompany westernisation. One of these is the relationship between industrial capitalism and private profit. As I pointed out earlier, it is frequently the merchants who are depicted as being the baddies in noodle westerns. According to Confucian ideals of the Tokugawa period, merchants were placed at the lowest end of the four social classes because, unlike the farming peasants and artisans above them, they did not produce anything. Rather, they dealt with the products of other people's labour and were seen to be interested in little more than profit. This method of making a living has always been regarded by the Japanese as somewhat suspect. Yamaga Sokō, for example, the mid-seventeenth-century neo-Confucian intellectual mentioned earlier, suggested that for the sage—and by implication the *samurai*—personal gain and a large salary should be as fleeting an attraction as 'a snowflake on a red hot stove' (Tsunoda *et al.* 1964: 394). In *jidaigeki*, it is the *samurai* who disregards this admonition by getting involved with merchants, and whose down-fall is finally brought about by his lust for gold, who is most roundly condemned. Now, given the role of the *samurai* in Tokugawa society as setting an example to the people, this atti-tude is understandable. What is not so easily grasped is the fact that money should still be seen as 'the root of all evil' in modern

Japan, where the production and marketing of commodity goods, together with the growth of the nation's GNP, have been publicly proclaimed as important social goals over the past thirty years.

Macfarlane (1985) has talked about the ambivalence of money and has suggested that money eliminates the concept of evil because it ushers in a world of moral confusion. While I am inclined to agree with the idea that money is morally confusing, I am not convinced that 'it is money, markets and market capitalism that eliminate absolute moralities' (p. 72). Confucian ethics, like the Protestant ethic, have always highly valued work, as can be seen in such phrases as *hataraku sugata wa utsukushii* ('how beautiful the figure of someone working'). This means that the division of labour is not seen as being necessarily 'wrong' in Japan, because group ideals at the company or factory level unite workers and managers. Work is especially good when it is done on behalf of others. A similar attitude prevails towards money, which *in itself* is seen as evil. Fujiwara Seika's comment made around the turn of the seventeenth century still holds good: 'Commerce is the business of selling and buying in order to bring profit to both parties. It is not to gain profit at the expense of others' (Tsunoda *et al.* 1964: 340). This attitude goes some way towards explaining why the Japanese 'economic miracle' has occurred and why, perhaps, our own economy is so depressed. Christianity warns us that the pursuit of money is evil, Confucianism stresses that people are allowed—indeed, ought—to make money, but that they should then put it to proper social use. Noodle westerns reinforce this ideal. They remind the present-day businessman that it is not just entrepreneurial skill that matters: he must make some contribution to the welfare of others (*cf.* Vogel 1963: 160). The continued emphasis on this attitude to money-making partly explains, I think, why modern businesses plough back their profits into sporting competitions, art exhibitions and other cultural activities. They must be seen to be making money for the benefit of the Japanese nation as a whole, not just for themselves.

Third, noodle westerns also touch on the problem of urbanisation and its accompanying impersonalisation. Urbanisation in Japan, of course, is not new. The *jidaigeki* depict society in Edo (present-day Tokyo), which by 1733 had a population of 1.4 million people and was probably the largest city in the world

(Yazaki 1968: 134). But Edo in Tokugawa times was somewhat different from Tokyo today. Starting from the shogun's castle, the city was carefully laid out, with feudal lords living in one area, *samurai* retainers in another and the common people in wards that were guarded and sealed off at night. What the noodle westerns portray, therefore, is a city of inherent order in which each citizen is allotted his station in life and knows how to act accordingly. They intimate that modern Tokyo-ites may end up in chaos if they fail to observe this order and ignore the personal connections (*tsukiai*) by which people organize their social relationships. Consequently, *jidaigeki* portray a society in which the anonymity of modern Western urban society does not exist. Not only do they emphasise the importance of kinship groups, neighbourhood associations and mutual friendship, but they also suggest that neither the sovereign nor the law is aloof, and that those who govern Japan always have their eyes and ears open to the needs of the people. However high their social status, rulers are at one with the ruled. Together they form a united group which is the Japanese nation.

At the same time, there is a neat oriental twist of fiction to make life coincide with fact. The urban society that is portrayed in the noodle western is that of the Edo townspeople (*chōnin*). It is the culture of the common people, and not that of the *samurai*, that is eventually held up as an example to present-day Japanese. Here some concession has had to be made to reality. The four-class system of *samurai*—peasant—artisan—merchant is sacrificed to some extent to a—I dare not say 'the'—notion of democracy. Just as one people's power can be another's Exide battery, so is democracy in Japan interpreted in a specifically Japanese manner, and so does it depend on the important principles of social obligation and human feeling, *giri* and *ninjō*.[8] . . .

Here we come face to face with the masked bandit of Japanese thought. Westernisation, capitalism and urban anonymity are three of the unacceptable faces of individualism that, unlike Batman or Dynatron rods, fails to do anybody any good at all. The Japanese are wary of the notion of individualism because they feel that its adoption will merely serve to lead Japan down the straight and narrow path to social chaos. In stressing the importance of familial relationships, therefore, *jidaigeki* are merely echoing the very real apprehension of intellectuals, businessmen and politicians. Anthropologists talk of the household group as being the basic element in Japanese social organisation; businessmen proudly proclaim that their company is 'one happy family'; and a recently-elected Prime Minister of Japan could make an inaugural 'policy' speech with the question: 'Wherein lies the happiness of the people? It is when the family hurry home and, joined around the dinner table, are together in an aura of contentment'.

'Good' and 'evil' conclusions

I have already suggested that Chu Hsi's metaphysical distinction between immaterial principle and material ether is paralleled in Japan by a social distinction between ties of obligation and spontaneity. What I wish to argue by way of conclusion is that an emphasis on either *giri* or *ninjō* leads social anthropologists to adopt one of two models by which to explain Japanese social organisation. Just as Neo-Confucian scholars of Tokugawa Japan emphasised *ri* or *ki*, and so came to interpretations of Japanese ethics that saw man as naturally good or naturally evil, so do modern anthropologists emphasise either a 'group' or 'social exchange' model of Japanese society and come to similar conclusions about the nature of Japanese social organisation through *giri* and *ninjō* (see Table 2).

Table 2

Group model	Social exchange model
li (*ri*) immaterial principle	*ch'i* (*ki*) material ether
keijijō, above shapes	*keijika*, below shapes
perfection	imperfection (desire *yoku*)
essential nature	physical nature
society	individual
giri, obligation	*ninjō*, spontaneity

It seems to me that, in Japanese anthropology (and, indeed, in Japanese studies in general), there are—although they may not realise it—followers of Mencius and followers of Hsun-tzu. Those who believe that Japanese society is essentially good adopt the group model, while those who believe it is evil adopt the model of social exchange. Needless to say, the Japanese themselves prefer to be seen as good and so tend to adopt the group model (as espoused by Nakane (1970), for example). At the same time, I suspect that foreigners studying Japan ultimately regard their own Christian societies as evil and look to Japan (as other anthropologists, indeed, look to other more 'primitive' societies (see Pratt 1986: 47–8) for the good that they themselves have never been able to experience back home.

This brings us back to a point made in the previous chapter about the perceived division between country and city in Japan. By emphasising in foreign peoples such traits as co-operation, lack of interest in material goods, non-violence, harmony and anything else that is noticeably lacking in western societies, anthropologists are guilty of indulging in what Clifford (1986: 113) refers to as 'salvage' ethnography. In fact, many of these ideals are part and parcel of the European notion of 'organic community', which itself stemmed from the Industrial Revolution and signified a *rural* community (Williams 1963: 252). In other words, like Japanese advertisers, anthropologists are themselves involved in a cultural debate over rural and urban societies.

We have already encountered this sense of the 'organic' when we looked at folk-craft aesthetics in Chapter 5, and one of the interesting things about Yanagi's concept of *mingei* is that it owes direct allegiance to the popular art theories put forward by William Morris in the latter half of the ninteenth century (Moeran 1984: 9–11). Morris himself, of course, was influenced by other social critics—like Carlyle—before him, and they all shared a vision of 'culture' as a 'whole way of life' as a result of their general experience of industrialism. Western anthropologists have themselves inherited the same literary tradition. Only, in their case, in an attempt to come to grips with this 'whole way of life', anthropologists have replaced the eighteenth-century village with various kinds of recent simple societies (Williams 1963: 229). Japan may not be one of these, but anthropologists, by focusing on a set of characteristics patently different from their own, treat the Japanese *as if* they were a primitive, exotic people. In this respect, they yearn for the Garden of Eden before the apple tree bore fruit.

Notes

1 This can be seen, for example, in the family morality of the extremely popular character, Sazaesan (see Tsurumi 1987: 114).

2 In the following paragraphs I have relied particularly on Chang (1957: 243–83) and Fung Yu-lan (1953: 533–71).

3 *Langue* differs from *li* in that it *can* be generative, but I still feel that the parallel is worth making.

4 The anthropological literature on hair and hairlessness suggests an equation between self-abandon and self-control, respectively. I find it interesting, therefore, that the notion of the shaven head seems frequently to connote evil, and sexuality, in films. Yul Brynner may have been a model of good behaviour in *The King and I*, but actors like Telly Savalas and Donald Pleasance frequently find themselves in the role of evil gangster, desperado, villain or spy. Balding academics should, perhaps, beware.

5 To some extent, of course, television dramas in the West use the same contrasts for the same didactic ends. In the noodle westerns, incidentally, baddies are almost invariably men, even though the Tendai and Shingon sects of Buddhism have taught that women are inherently evil and are able to attain salvation only by first being reborn as men. In fifteenth-century Japan women were accused of being agents of the devil whose aim was to prevent their husbands from following the way of the Buddha (*cf.* Paulson 1976: 9).

6 Some might think that the reference here to a slightly obscure British upper-middle-class children's story is out of place in a book such as this, but my reason for including it stems from more than a desire to betray my childhood reading habits. In many ways, the world of Pooh Bear is a Confucian world of the kind idealised in Japanese noodle westerns. It may not be so violent, perhaps, but its actors are basically kind and generous, and soon recognise the errors of their ways when they do, inadvertently, like Owl, upset their neighbours. They live in a harmony with one another, which we, and the Japanese, find impossible to emulate in real life.

7 One might note here the frequency with which such phrases as 'I have been utterly indebted to you' (*sukkari o-sewa ni narimashita*) and 'the return of obligation' (*ongaeshi ni*) occur.

8 It is of interest to note here that the Japanese had no word for 'democracy' until they came into contact with the West, whereupon they hit upon the loan creation *minshushugi*. Recently, however, an English loanword, *demokurashī*, has come into use. *Minshushugi* now refers to a specifically 'Japanese' style of democracy and has positive connotations; *demokurashī* refers to Western-style parliamentary rule and has somewhat negative connotations.

11

Jidaigeki, yakuza
and 'eroduction' films

Introduction

Although Westerners may look upon Japan with a certain sense of misconstrued exoticism, and see its people as 'primitive' and 'childlike',[1] not everyone is taken in by the veneer of harmony and group identification. Critics of Japanese film and popular culture, for example, have had occasion to comment upon the nihilism and violence often found therein. However, since anthropologists dealing with Japan have rarely been interested in film, and since film critics are rarely interested in Japanese social organisation, the paradox between an ideology based on harmony and a popular culture which, noodle westerns notwithstanding, makes much of unharmonious activities has rarely been addressed. Buruma (1984) has suggested that the sort of violence alluded to in the following sections of this chapter provides an outlet by which Japanese society is made safer, and that the kinds of sadism, masochism, torture, and other forms of violence found in films and popular literature, are in effect mere fantasies of a people forced in their everyday lives to be gentle and meek. Violence is, in short, seen to be no more than a reversal of normal, everyday behaviour (behaviour that is very much along the lines of the group model)—'a direct result of being made to conform to such a strict and limiting code of normality' (1984: 225).

While there is clearly some truth in this argument, I feel that there is more to the explanation than a functionalist approach which argues that a society needs an alternative ideology in order that otherwise repressed feelings of aggression might emerge in some socially acceptable form. My own research suggests that violence in Japanese society cannot be separated from attitudes towards sex, death and beauty, and that all of these may be connected with concepts of time and space. Certainly, the Japanese do not introduce scenes of women having their bellies ripped open, or of men slashing one another to gory death, merely to show what their society might be like if people did not obey the principles of harmony and group commitment espoused by politicians, company directors and educationalists. They do so in an attempt to overcome, firstly, the concept of time, and secondly, that of space as represented by notions of self and other. By coming to terms with time, the Japanese are able to go beyond Western acculturation and return to a foetal sense of 'Japaneseness'. An awareness of what it means to be 'Japanese' simultaneously leads to an emphasis on group ideals and harmony in Japanese society and denies that there is any distance between 'self' and 'other'. In short, violence—together with sex, death and the appreciation of beauty—*is* a means towards supporting social ideals, but not quite for the reasons suggested hitherto.

Jidaigeki, yakuza and 'eroduction' films

One of the characteristics of the Japanese film industry is that films are readily categorised into types, depending on their subject matter. Thus we find a distinction made between types of hero/heroine portrayed (e.g. the *hahamono* 'mother' films, and *tsumamono* 'wife' films); between films depicting certain groups in Japanese society (e.g. the *rumpenmono* 'vagrant' films, *taiyōzokumono* 'sun tribe' youth gang films, and *sararimanmono* 'salary man' films); between differences in historical settings (e.g. *Meijimono, Meiji* Period films (1868–1912), and *Taishōmono*, Taisho Period film (1912–26)).

The most obvious historical distinction is that drawn between *gendaimono*, 'modern' films, and *jidaigeki*, 'period' films. *Jidaigeki* refers to all films whose stories take place prior to the Meiji Restoration in 1868 and which therefore deal with Japanese society prior to its westernisation. *Gendaimono* refers to all films whose action takes place after the Meiji Restoration. It is, therefore, Japan's official break with feudalism and its first contacts with the west which mark the dividing line between 'period' and 'modern' films.

The *jidaigeki* themselves subsume a further subdivision, known as *chanbara*. Whereas *jidaigeki* can range in time right back to the Heian Period (794–1185) or even earlier, *chanbara* deal almost exclusively with the Tokugawa Period (1603–1868). This distinction is not, however, entirely based on historical periods. Many— but not all (e.g. Anderson and Richie 1959: 59–62)—film critics regard *jidaigeki* as serious art, in which directors attempt to discover what is of unique value in Japanese history, and how this uniqueness should be preserved. In these films, we find that social norms are in fact frequently questioned, as heroes are made to work out for themselves what it is that they should believe and how they should live. In this respect, *jidaigeki* differ from the kind of escapist entertainment discussed in the previous chapter— the noodle westerns, or *chanbara*—which unthinkingly accept the *status quo* and thereby act as what Mellon (1976; 116) calls 'the touchstone of authoritarian art'.

The *jidaigeki* probably went through their golden age in the two decades before the Pacific War. It has been suggested that one reason for their popularity then lies in the fact that the past was seen as less threatening an arena in which to discuss social problems. Directors could avoid being seen—by either the military regime or by the film companies—as dissidents, if they set their plots in a dim and distant past. At the same time, it seems unlikely that these ploys fooled the audiences. In this way, political authority, the market and the general public were all satisfied. Attacking present-day society by means of the *jidaigeki* was a form of ritualised dissent in a society which frowned upon open criticism (Mellen 1976: 85–6). In spite of my earlier conclusions, therefore, it can be seen that popular culture does not necessarily *always* toe the party line.

This searching in the past to answer problems of the present did have its unexpected results. The pre-war military government did not regard the *jidaigeki* as much of a threat to the social order; yet the post-war American Occupation forces tried to get rid of the genre because they thought it too chauvinistic and militaristic. The Americans were not, however, very successful in this, and the *jidaigeki* came back into fashion in the mid-1950s—at a time when the Japanese were going through an economic boom and were, at the same time, beginning to turn back to their old traditions in a renewed identity crisis. Ironically, perhaps, American disapproval of the period films led to Japanese directors concentrating their attention on the *yakuza* genre, in which gangsters acted as modern-day *samurai*, behaving according to 'feudal' values, and bringing each film to a rousing climax with bloody sword-play and dagger-throwing. We thus find in the *yakuza* genre the whole gamut of Tokugawa period values re-emerging in present-day industrial society.

Part of the emphasis on the production of *yakuza* and *jidaigeki* lies in the situation in which the Japanese film industry found itself in the 1950s. Not only were production costs rising, but so were admission charges. Television was booming in popularity and, as a result, attracting more and more advertising. In order to combat all this, in 1952 the cinemas began showing double features, and major companies found that they were being required to turn out approximately one feature a week to keep the cinemas supplied. The fastest method of production, of course, was the action picture in which a series of films could be produced with the same sets, costumes and even actors (Anderson and Richie 1959: 245).

Kyoto rapidly became the centre for the production of *jidaigeki*, and Tokyo that of *yakuza* films, of which something like 1500 were made in the decade lasting from the mid-1960s to the mid-1970s (Tucker 1973: 127). In an attempt to attract a wider audience, which was rapidly decreasing because of the popularity of television, film directors stuck to the idea of limited plots characterised by violence and bloodshed. From the *yakuza* films developed a whole range about 'discontented youth, school drop-outs, drug addicts and tormented young love ... Narcotics, prostitution, extortion and revenge became the staple diet. Studios went to extreme lengths to capture the market in these films, some even using ex-gangsters as stars' (Tucker: 123).[2] In the mid-60s, two-thirds to three-quarters of all films produced were of the *yakuza* type. By the 1970s, the same percentage of films made in Japan were 'eroductions', or 'pink' films. These started out as low-budget one-hour films in which out-of-work models, actors, and even volunteers took part. They were immensely successful, if only because television could not show such erotic scenes and hence were unable to compete with them.

At the same time, the *yakuza* films became highly charged with sexual elements, so that we can see in the development of these three genres of Japanese film—the *jidaigeki, yakuza* and 'eroduction'—the emergence of a form of popular culture which emphasised both sex and violence. One example from many can be seen in Masumura Yasuzō's *The Red Angel* (1966), where the erotic development of a young woman is closely tied up with her experience as a nurse in a field hospital, and with her confrontation with the horrors of violent and bloody death.

Violence, sex, death and beauty

One aspect of violence in Japanese films is the extent to which, in both the *jidaigeki* and *yakuza* genres, killing seems to go on for the sake of killing and details of slaughter are lovingly observed. Long before *The Wild Bunch*, Japanese directors were filming slow-motion shots of flesh exploding under the impact of bullets, and they also developed somewhat gruesome forms of make-up and special effects. We can see limbs being cut off and bodies hewn in two, and make-up artists have now developed a technique whereby a sword will first appear to slash a man's face before— two or three seconds later—a razor-like cut will open up and the victim's blood begin to flow (Tucker 1973: 112).[3]

Some critics, such as Anderson and Richie (1959: 318), are not so impressed with the technical mastery of Japanese film makers in their portrayal of violence. 'Pointless killing is one of the main features of the Japanese film ... the feeling of the cheapness of life is inescapable ... Japanese films also tend to accentuate the attendant gore. Gushing blood, open wounds and the like abound ... There are also all kinds of torture and various varieties of suicide. Often the violence goes beyond the bounds of plot necessity.'

This view is shared by Mellen. Bloodshed pervades the *chanbara*, she says, quite independently of any rationale in the plots, which act as occasions for violence in much the same way as in pornography films they act as occasions for sexuality. 'In *chan-*

bara the charge, arousal, and catharsis derived from the gore and blood-letting are equally orgasmic. The violence of the *chanbara* is a sexual surrogate and also an emblem of sensuality in a repressed culture' (Mellen 1976: 118).

While I shall return to the relationship between repression and violence later on, we should note here that sex has always figured strongly in Japanese art and literature, and that a number of visual and poetic metaphors have been adopted into the semiotics of Japanese film (for example, the transience of life and youth seen in the falling of the cherry blossoms; mountain waterfalls signifying passion; the Buddhist notion of impurity seen in the clouds of dust surrounding so many of Kurosawa's battle scenes, and in Ichikawa Kon's *The Harp of Burma* (1956) with its opening epitaph: 'Blood red are the soil and peaks of Burma').

In art, we find that many of Japan's greatest artists did work which we in the West might well label 'pornographic'. Pornography was widely prevalent and goes back to tenth-century drawings known as *warai-e*, which depicted monks and abbots indulging in all sorts of sexual activities (Buruma 1984: 55). Erotic pillow books used to be given to young brides as early as the Heian Period, even though it is only in recent post-war decades that young people have been seen holding hands—let alone kissing—in public.[4] Other artists indulged in sadism. The woodblock print artist Kuniyoshi, for example, and his pupil Yoshitoshi, portrayed women being tortured—as did the Edo Period artist, Ekin.

The relationship between sex and death is a frequent feature of Japanese literature, where we find parallels with Bataille's notion that eroticism is the joy of life pushed to the point of death (Bataille 1965)—the union of *eros* and *thanatos*. Tanizaki Junichirō, for example, in his 1962 *Diary of a Mad Old Man (Futen Rōjin Nikki)*, describes the way in which his hero—like many others in this author's work, a foot fetishist—feels his blood pressure rise whenever his daughter-in-law allows him to lick her feet. 'The thought of really dying did frighten me. I tried to calm myself down, telling myself not to get excited. The strange thing is, however, that I never stopped sucking her feet. I couldn't stop. The more I sought to stop, the harder I sucked, like an idiot. Thinking I was going to die, I still kept on sucking. Fear and excitement and pleasure came in turns' (quoted in Buruma 1984:

49). This theme is echoed in another of Tanizaki's novels, *The Key (Kagi)*, made into a film directed by Ichikawa in 1959 (and titled in English *The Odd Obsession*). The hero has a stroke while making love to his wife, who (in the film) then tempts him once more by stripping in front of him—enough to raise his blood pressure and cause him to die.

Another modern author to describe the relationship between sex and death in a number of works was Mishima Yukio. In *Patriotism (Yūkoku)*, based on the 26 February 1936 Incident, in which a number of important political and military figures were murdered by army rebels, Mishima describes a lieutenant who did not take part in the assassinations and who decided to commit suicide rather than have to take action against those of his friends who had participated. As he lies on a mattress waiting to make love to his wife for the last time, he thinks about the whole affair: 'Was it death he was now waiting for? Or a wild ecstasy of the senses? The two seemed to overlap, almost as if the object of his bodily desire was death itself. But, however that might be, it was certain that never before had the lieutenant tasted such total freedom' (quoted in Buruma 1984: 165).

Here we have echoes of Kabuki theatre where a favourite theme is that of lovers dying together—something which is seen by the Japanese as the supreme form of sexual ecstasy. The choice of death is, in an ordered society, perhaps the only moment in which an individual can attain true liberation.

Mishima is, in fact, one of Japan's more interesting modern writers in that he acted out in real life what he frequently alluded to in his fiction and essays. By committing the *samurai's* ritual act of *seppuku*, Mishima forced the Japanese to consider—if but briefly—the meaning of death in a modern society whose major premise is that it is best to live as long as possible (Mishima 1977: 27). Before disembowelling himself in the headquarters of the Japanese Self-Defence Force, he shouted down from the balcony to those assembled below: 'Have you studied *Bu*? Do you understand the way of the sword? What does the sword mean to a Japanese? ...I ask you. Are *you* men? Are you *bushi* (warriors)?' (quoted in Scott-Stokes 1974: 47).

In this context, one of Mishima's more interesting works is *The Way of the Samurai*, his commentary on the early-eighteenth-century work on this theme—*Hagakure (Hidden Leaves)*—by the Nabeshima clan retainer, Yamamoto Jōchō. Concerned that modern Japanese society was slipping into an 'age of performing artists', in which baseball players and television pop stars were the only people to get public attention, Mishima objected to the fact that human beings had ceased to be 'total human personalities' and were 'reduced to a kind of skilled puppet'. What one should do, he claimed, was 'live beautifully and die beautifully' (Mishima 1977: 21–2).

Mishima cites the *Hagakure* as a splendid example of 'a living philosophy that holds life and death as the two sides of one shield' (p. 42). In it he discovers for himself the *Hagakure*'s notion that: 'The way of the samurai is death. Human life lasts but an instant. One should spend it doing what one pleases. In this world fleeting as a dream, to live in misery doing what one dislikes is foolishness.'

The morality of the *samurai*—and, of course, of the *jidaigeki* and *yakuza* films—is a supremely male view of morality.[5] Indeed, the values of the *yakuza* gangsters are essentially a reassertion of patriarchal supremacy (Mellen 1976: 126) in a society which has gradually become more 'feminine' in its ways, with Westernisation and peace (*cf.* Mishima 1977: 18). Here, what I wish to point to is the fact that morality in the *Hagakure* is determined by aesthetics. 'What is beautiful must be strong, vivid and brimming with energy. This is the first principle: the second is that what is moral must be beautiful' (1977: 84). There is a nice circle of ideas here in which beauty = strength = death = morality = beauty.

Death is seen to be one of the purest acts man can carry out. And the emphasis here is on manliness. In many respects, it is the relationship between man and man, rather than between man and woman, which is the focus of much of Japanese literature and popular culture. In such epic tales as the story of the *Forty-seven Rōnin*, who avenged the death of their feudal lord and then committed suicide, we find that emotional involvements with women are ignored. As Nakane (1970: 71n.) has pointed out, in the fedual period men were so bent on devotion to their masters that they had very little time left to consider women. Not only this, but this kind of '*samurai* mentality' still permeates modern Japanese life.

In both the *jidaigeki* and *yakuza* films, we see a male-centred world in which the only meaningful relationships are those among men (Mellen 1976: 126). We find a kind of 'homosexual chivalry' based on death. Movie heroes often 'perish together in a splendidly suicidal last stand against an impossible majority of enemies. Often this orgasmic finale is the only time one sees them looking happy' (Buruma 1984: 129). This, too, is the stock image of the *kamikaze* pilot who smilingly plunges his plane in its steep dive to destruction.

This cult of death is closely connected with youth, for 'death is the only pure and thus fitting end to the perfection of youth' (1984: 131).⁶ This may explain, perhaps, why the Japanese like to keep their trees from growing by clipping them into miniature shrubs (*bonsai*); or why they see the cherry blossoms as a fleeting moment of purity, prior to the growth of leaves; or why they have cultivated the concept of *bishōnen*, androgynous youths, who by the very fragility of their beauty remind us of impermanence and death; or why Mishima can write that the higher, spiritual emotion for a Japanese is love of one man for another.

In other words, death is here the prevention of ugliness, and in this respect it is almost the reverse of the kinds of dualities discussed by Needham (1973). Certainly, in Japan, none of the concepts of death, sex or violence discussed here can be dealt with in terms of neat oppositional categories. Death is, for Mishima, 'an image . . . beyond which there exists a spring of pure water, from which tiny streams are continuously pouring their pure waters into this world' (Mishima 1977: 100). Here one cannot help comparing the *jidaigeki* or *yakuza* films with such rituals as the Spanish bullfight (*cf.* Marvin 1986), where the death of the bull at the hand of the *matador* functions as a kind of purification.⁷ In many films, the death of the *samurai* or gangster hero is just as inevitable and serves much the same purpose (*cf.* Buruma 1984: 171).

This notion of purity comes up once more in pornography and 'eroduction' films where torture is seen by some Japanese critics as a kind of 'purification ceremony'. Usually the victims in these films are women and, according to Shintō and Buddhist beliefs, women are basically impure because of the association of menstrual blood with pollution. Their sexuality, however, can be purified through rape and, in the eroduction films, we find that victims are such

169

innocent symbols as uniformed schoolgirls, nurses, or newly married housewives, who almost invariably become attracted to their rapists—and by this attraction reveal their inherent impurity (1984: 59).[8] At the same time, when intercourse takes place in most of these films, the man remains more or less fully clothed, while making use of such penis substitutes as whips, candles, pistols and shoe horns. To some extent this probably reveals a Japanese male anxiety of masculine inadequacy, and it is interesting to note that women in films—and in art in general—are frequently depicted as mother figures who end up comforting their aggressors once the latter confess their fear of sexual impotence. Women are seen to be the physical, and men the spiritual sufferers (1984: 61).

This might seem like an inconsistency, but the relationship here between men and women is, I would argue, logical. On the one hand, it seems as though rape defines women as 'bad', as having some innate sexual desire which is aroused by their being ravished. And yet, on the other, we find that women comfort their lovers, and become the good wives and mothers (*ryōsai kenbo*) that Japanese society expects of them. We thus end up with a nice structuralist formula along the lines of:

> male sexual excess : male sexual privation
> ::
> female impurity : female purity
> (as whore) (as mother)

This can be seen more clearly, perhaps, below:

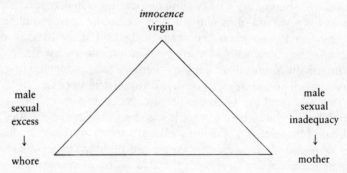

One point to be made about sex in general is that, from early times, it was the 'play' (*asobi*) involved in courtship or visits to brothels which was seen to be exciting, rather than the act of intercourse itself. Thus we find aristocratic men of the Heian Court peering through fences, trying to catch a brief glimpse of their loved ones, or exchanging melancholy poems with women whom they had perhaps seen but briefly in the shadows of a tree-lined garden. Much later on, in the Edo Period, men went to the 'floating world' (*ukiyo*) of Yoshiwara, the pleasure quarters of Tokyo (old Edo), and there dallied with courtesans who would entertain them with singing, dancing and any number of child-like games (*cf.* Dalby 1983: 139–61). Thus, 'human passion and its physical expression were not controlled by an abstract moral code, whether of chivalry or sin, but by aesthetics, by decorum for its own sake. Love was a kind of art for art's sake, an exquisite piece of theatre' (Buruma 1984: 78; *cf.* Dalby 1983: 216–17). In Japan, love and death, sex and violence, end up as works of art. Indeed, in the case of gangsters, their bodies *are* works of art, for they sport 'tatoos, painfully carved on their skins from the neck to the knees—sometimes even to the ankles. One can imagine their capacity, indeed their gluttony for pain' (Buruma, 184).[9] It is hardly surprising in this context to find that the craft of making swords has also been regarded as little short of a fine art in Japan. Aesthetics ends up not simply as the ritual purifier but as a de-lineator of the means by which such purification will take place.

Nihilism? Or the conquering of time and space?

If it is more on aesthetic, than purely ethical, grounds that the heroes of the *jidaigeki* and *yakuza* films are to be judged, we must also take account of the fact that they are trying to resolve that conflict of ideals brought on by Japan's modernisation over the past century, and referred to in the previous chapter, as well as elsewhere in this book. Is the individualism apparently denied by noodle westerns, advertising and the language of modernity possible in Japanese cinema?

It is perhaps not surprising to find that one form taken by individualism in films is that of nihilism, where all traditional beliefs are rejected and a doctrine of the purely negative is espoused. Richie (1982: 188) remarks that:

> Perhaps because Japanese society is so oppressive, liberation can take the extreme form of total nihilism. Nihilism as a course of action certainly began after the repressive Tokugawa government attained control. Collective big business in Japan still retains many features of that feudal period, and perhaps as a consequence the attractions of nihilism remain. Even in a picture such as *Samurai Rebellion* ... the sheer joy of negation (killing people, destroying houses) can be seen as at least a part of the motivation for the action.

Again:'In films such as *The Pornographers* ... the director (Imamura Shōhei) is really celebrating a completely amoral, vital, and overflowing rejection of Japanese collective beliefs' (p. 188).

While the first nihilistic heroes of the cinema emerged in *jidai-geki* as early as 1927 (Anderson and Richie 1959: 137), Richie argues that the new post-war nihilism was brought on by the fact that by the 1960s Japan had become an affluent and leisure-oriented society which ignored the traditional values based on a Confucian work ethic (Richie 1982: 190). Both the *jidaigeki* and the *yakuza* films which continued—on the surface at least—to protray in modern form the 'soul of the warrior', made use of the past as a means of coming to terms with the present. In this respect, many directors set their films in the past—not to praise or exalt a set of feudal values, but 'rather to uncover a route of escape from the rigid, restrictive, if compelling, definition of what it means to be a Japanese—a code which has been damaging to the individual and demeaning to the national dignity' (Mellen 1976: 59). To some extent, then, they share with Mishima 'the idea that a return to the traditions of old Japan, when it was a primitive island insulated from the rest of the world, would allow a revitalization of the culture' (1976: 10).[10]

What is of interest here is that in Japan every new 'religious' creed appears to have brought in its wake a spate of pornography and/or violence. The tenth-century *warai-e* drawings of monks and abbots indulging in various kinds of sexual activities were produced soon after the rise to power of Buddhism. The next major stage in pornography production was during the Edo Period when neo-Confucianism was adopted and imposed by the ruling shogunate. Now it is Westernisation and an essentially Christian morality to which Japan has to some extent succumbed as it pursues its quest for perfection in the system of industrial capitalism. This point ties up with Girard's argument that it is religion which keeps man's violence within bounds—religion being defined as 'that obscurity that surrounds man's efforts to defend himself by curative or preventative means against his own violence' (1977: 23).

There are two points that I would like to make by way of parenthesis here. The first is that the way in which women fall in love with their rapists in modern pornographic films, mentioned earlier, could in some respects be seen as a metaphor for Japan itself, as—over the centuries—it has adulatingly adopted each new wave of culture from, first, the Asian continent and now, the west. The second stems from Girard's argument (1977: 115) that there are both 'good' and 'bad' forms of violence, that violence is 'good' when it is sacrificial, and that a destructive cycle of violence can only come to an end when it is directed against a surrogate victim (p. 93). While Girard's argument centres on, and is illustrated by, classical mythology, I believe that—in the case of Japanese society—the 'surrogate victim' is in fact westernisation. Violence in Japan is, therefore, directed towards maintaining Japanese values. In this respect it does not operate 'without reason' (p. 46) so much as *against* reason, for these values, as I pointed out in Chapter 4, are ultimately concerned to go beyond the comprehensibility of logic and the mind (a point to which I shall return below). 'Good' violence is sacrificial because it brings about selflessness, and selflessness is harmonious in that it maintains group ideals.

The sense of nihilism that arises from the clash of two differing systems of thought is also connected with the long-felt Japanese sense of transience, or impermanence (*mujō*). We have already seen this underlying the idea of purity of youth, and in Mishima's notion (a notion shared by a long line of writers from Lady Murasaki onwards) that the world is but a fleeting dream. In aesthetic terms, this transience has been alluded to as *mono no aware*, or the 'pathos of things', whereby beauty is linked with sadness at the natural evanescence of our lives and of the world in general.[11]

Above all, the idea of impermanence suggests the fragility of *time*, and it is time, I would suggest, which lies at the heart of this strange quartet of violence, sex, death and beauty. Again, it is Mishima who makes the point: 'Time changes human beings, makes them inconsistent and opportunistic, makes them degenerate or, in a very few cases, improve. However, if one assumes that humanity is always facing death, and that there is no truth except from moment to moment, then the process of time does not merit the respect we accord it.' (1977: 43).

It seems to me that everything about *jidaigeki* and *yakuza* films is an attempt to stop time. On the surface, this is obvious. *Jidaigeki* are period dramas whose plots take place entirely in (pre)feudal Japan. The present is thus collapsed into the past. Japanese filmmakers also perform acts of 'salvage'.

At the same time we should note that, in both the martial and aesthetic arts, it is the principle of selflessness which is extolled. Here the influence of Zen Buddhism is, of course, very strong. The practitioner of an art is invited to be at one with the object s/he produces. We have seen this in Yanagi Sōetsu's notion of *chokkan*, or 'direct perception'. Similarly, in swordsmanship, the *samurai* seeks to lose all consciousness of his self, like the high school baseball pitcher to be 'without heart' (*mushin*), to be at one with his surroundings. The famous Edo Period swordsman and painter, Miyamoto Musashi, has written about this in his *Book of Five Rings*: 'The Book of the Void. By void I mean that which has no beginning and no end. Attaining this principle means not attaining the principle. The Way of strategy is the Way of Nature. When you appreciate the power of nature, knowing the rhythm of any situation, you will be able to hit the enemy naturally and strike naturally. All this is the Way of the Void' (Miyamoto 1974: 44).

This notion of selflessness demands that man—and it is 'man' rather than 'woman'—go beyond his thinking self and intuitively grasp a spiritual nothingness which is beyond dualities of good and bad, right and wrong, beauty and ugliness. In this respect, it can be said to be anti-language. Yet language does in many respects make us aware of time (cf. Bloch 1977: 283). In Japan— and doubtless in many other societies, too—the appreciation of beauty, the sexual climax and the attainment of selflessness when face to face with death, are all moments when language is driven from man's mind and time is conquered. It is only at such moments perhaps that the Japanese can overcome the irrevocable march of history, only then that they can solve the inherent conflict between individual desires and group constraints. The conquering of time simultaneously becomes the conquering of the space between self and other.

Notes

1 I have developed this theme in 'The Debris of Civilization: popular art movements in England and Japan', a paper delivered at 'The Occident and the Orient' conference held at the Humanities Research Centre, Australian National-al University, in July 1987.

2 One of the foremost producers of *yakuza* films. Taoka Mitsuru, is himself the son of a powerful gangland boss, Taoka Kazuo, who was killed by a rival gang in 1981.

3 Some of the emphasis on visual effects in Japanese films may be due to a tendency for the Japanese to depend on the eye, rather than the ear, when it comes to aesthetic sensibility.

4 The first kiss on Japanese film was screened on 23 May 1946 in two films which opened on the same day: Chiba Yasuki's *A Certain Night's Kiss (Aru yo no seppun)*, and Sasaki Yasuki's *Twenty Year Old Youth (Hatachi no sieshun)*. Public reaction centred on such questions as: was it commercial or artistic motivation which prompted the filming of a kiss? Was there any sexual meaning in a kiss? Was a kiss 'Japanese' or not? Was a kiss hygienic or not? (Anderson and Richie 1959: 176). Kyō Machiko was 'the first actress to have public attention drawn to her sex appeal' (1959: 232) in the early 1950s: Yamamoto Satsuyo was the first actress to appear on the screen nude, in 1956.

5 As will be discussed below, in Japanese film and literature there is a close association between masculinity, beauty and the exaltation of death, on the one hand, and femininity, torture and sexuality, on the other. One question which has not been addressed in this chapter, but which merits consideration, is whether in Japan, as well as elsewhere, there is not 'some half-suppressed desire to place the blame for all forms of violence on women' (Girard 1977: 36).

6 My colleague, David Parkin, who was kind enough to read through and comment on an earlier draft of this chapter, has drawn my attention to the fact that there is a parallel between the cult of death and youth in Japan and the killing of the diving king before his powers wane in certain African kingdoms.

7 Clearly, the comparison could be taken much further. The linking of violence with sex, death and beauty is immediately reminiscent of the work of authors like Garcia Lorca and Hemingway, as well as such writers as Sade, Genet and Camus. The 'aestheticisation' of violence would appear to be a characteristic particularly common in both French and Japanese modern literature.

8 Buruma (1984: 60) goes on to compare the symbolisation of pollution in films with the form of certain ancient Shintō ceremonies.

9 For a full historical account and structural analysis of Japanese tatooing, see Van Gulik 1982.
10 Here again, there is ambivalence, in that nihilism offers the individual an almost frightening liberation, while she or he is at the same time oppressed by feudal values. It is, therefore, difficult to talk of death and violence in terms of clear-cut oppositions which tend to offer the mind an easy theoretical escape from what is in fact a complicated existential 'reality'.
11 Harries (1989) has recently suggested that *aware* is the structural equivalent of the Western sense of 'tragedy'.

Conclusion:
Japanese orientalism

Introduction

In this book, I have made use of linguistic, semiotic and anthropological theories to examine certain aspects of popular culture in contemporary Japan. In many respects, the book only scratches at the surface of Japanese society's numerous cultural forms, but I have tried to focus throughout on two things in particular: firstly, the role of *language* in popular culture; and secondly, the role of ideology in Japanese *society*. My findings here have led me to make a number of statements about the role of anthropology in the promulgation of this ideology, which is itself, it would seem, to some extent dependent on Japan's response to the West. It is now time to recap the main arguments put forward in the preceding chapters and to try to disentangle the complicated relationship that exists between Western images of Japan, anthropologists' images of Japan, and Japanese images of their own society and culture.

Language, society and popular culture

First of all, let us start by looking at the Japanese language itself. I have argued that, whereas Western languages—specifically English—seem to prefer to make use of grammatical structures when creating a 'discourse', Japanese is more likely to make use of lexical categories—specifically, keywords. There are implications here, of course, for those scholars of Western linguistics who have emphasised the role of *grammatical structures* in their theoretical conclusions. However, the question asked in this book is whether keywords serve to support the *status quo* or invite change. As we have already seen, in some contexts they stifle the exchange and expression of new ideas; in others, precisely because they are conceptually condensed and lexically and semantically predictable, they enable new meanings to be smuggled in. Keywords, like popular culture itself, cannot be 'innocent'. As we have seen with the potters of Sarayama, people are always engaged in a battle for the successful manipulation of keywords. Those who control language ultimately control their social environment.

A second problem that we encountered when describing the workings of the Japanese language was: does it reinforce, or break down, social divisions? In some areas, such as the use of personal referents or role terms, we saw that the opposition between 'self' and 'other' was neatly overcome and an 'in-group' solidarity created. This idea was paralleled in my discussion of the role of violence in Japanese films, where I suggested that the aim was to overcome such dualities as 'self' and 'other', 'individual' and 'group', 'mind' and 'body', and so on. Here, indeed, the Japanese are invited to enter a spiritual vacuum in which language itself finally disappears. Ideally, they thereby become Beckettian characters who achieve final absolution from words.

But not all popular cultural forms support this total 'oneness' of the (non)self. It is clear that there *are* social divisions in Japanese society and that these cannot be easily dismissed. One of these depends on *age*. We saw in my description of *sake* drinking the way in which a younger generation of men made use of a popular cultural form to question the authority of a group of elders, and that there was a set of oppositions that arraigned age, authority, public speech and form, on the one hand, against youth, power, private speech and content, on the other. Some of these oppositions came up again in my discussion of tourist brochures, which put forward a 'language of modernity' that set leisure against the old work ethic, and internationalism against the old values of 'Japaneseness'. In this context, the aesthetic cult of death found in *yakuza* and *jidai̧ eki* films takes on intriguing significance. It will be recalled that this cult focused on *youth*, and I would suggest that, by handing over to the young the privilege of being able to perform the perfect sacrifice to the 'true' values of Japan, the elder generation is able to maintain overall control of the myth-making process. Here we have an interesting interpretation of the norm of social reciprocity, or—in common Japanese parlance—*gibu ando tēki*.

Another social division that occurred time and time again in my discussion of popular culture was that of *gender*. Not only did we see that the 'group' or *samurai* model of Japanese society was primarily a *male*-oriented model; women were frequently portrayed as being 'polluted' unless they took on the role of 'good wife and wise mother' (*ryōsai kenbo*). Even where some popular cultural forms—such as advertising—appeared to question this stereotypic role, we found that in fact the underlying ideology supported it. For example, a survey of brochures suggested that young women might be freed from social constraints by participating in foreign tourism. In fact, however, along with the traditional pursuits of tea ceremony and *ikebana* flower arrangement, such tourism has come to be included as a prerequisite for a good wife and wise mother, so that by going abroad young women are in fact making themselves more acceptable within the marriage market.

Finally, we come to social division by *status*. We first encountered this in my explanation of Japanese honorifics, where I pointed out that because of the principles of 'out-groupness', position, age and sex, it was impossible for a Japanese speaker to use language neutrally. The speaker always ended up being either 'higher' or 'lower' than the person to whom s/he was speaking. And yet at the same time, the social ideal put forward by the Japanese has been that people act in the framework of a 'group', and that this sense of 'groupness' serves to overcome differences in social status. The fact that the group model is in fact an *elite* model, based upon *samurai* values, is carefully overlooked.

Not surprisingly, we find this apparent contradiction taken up by various forms of popular culture. 'Noodle westerns', for example, basically portray an urban, *chōnin* culture in which those of extremely high status are seen to mix with those of the lowest social order. Leaders are leaders precisely because they are able to 'lower' themselves and thereby come to understand the problems of those whom they govern. This myth is, of course, also presented in the prevalent media image of the Japanese corporation in which managers are said to be 'equal' with their workers—sharing the same uniform, the same work space, even to some extent the same job. Status differences may exist, but, as we saw in the case of honorific usage where nobody is *absolutely* superior or inferior, social divisions are blurred in such a way that the Japanese really do seem to be one happy 'family'.

Here we come to a third set of problems, centring on Japan's adoption of, and response to, industrial capitalism. One of the *sine qua non*s of Marxist theory has been the development of social classes in those societies practising the capitalist mode of production. In postwar Japan, however, much has been said to support the idea that consciousness of social class is weak. While there is now clear evidence that proves such assumptions wrong (*cf.* Rohlen 1983: 310–12), the ideals put forward by popular culture uphold the myth that the division of labour does not necessarily give rise to a breakdown in social cohesion. That Japanese capitalism is 'different' can also be seen in the way in which attitudes towards money-making are displayed in the 'noodle westerns'. One does not make a profit at the expense of, but *on behalf of*, others.

Thus society, as it is presented through popular culture, is for the most part a coherent and 'organic' entity. The Western concept of individualism is generally seen to be irrelevant to Japanese industrial capitalism, or else accepted only where it is socially beneficial (in other words, where people clearly act as individuals *for* others). In this way, the intricate web of typically Japanese social relationships (supported by ideals such as *giri* and *ninjō*) apparently remains uncontaminated by industrialisation. Where modernisation does affect society, as we saw with the potters of Sarayama, there is a strong ideological bias in favour of a previous, 'better' way of life. Co-operation among individuals is 'good' and promotes 'beauty'; the breakdown of such co-operation is 'bad' and gives rise to ugliness. Social organisation thus becomes the focus of both ethics and aesthetics.

A second aspect of industrialisation is urbanisation. I have argued that a major source of the Japanese emphasis on nature is to be found in the country's increasingly urban population. This may well provide a second explanation for *jidaigeki*'s emphasising *chōnin* culture. Noodle westerns present an ordered urban society. At the same time, however, by praising the virtues seen to exist in nature (*cf.* tourism or folk crafts), urbanites are in effect measuring the extent to which Japanese culture has progressed—especially since the end of the Pacific War. Here we find that the countryside, together with all its values of 'tradition', 'harmony', 'co-operation' and 'groupness', is exoticised by those living in urban surroundings that are hardly harmonious in their modernity or conducive to small group cooperation. We have seen this attitude expressed in brochures for domestic tourism, in advertising slogans, and folk crafts, where nature becomes the flip side of culture on the popular cultural coin.

Japan and the West

This leads me to my final theme of Japan *vis-à-vis* the West. In many respects, the way in which urban Japanese behave towards their country cousins is no different from the way that we in Europe, or the United States, behave towards those living in what remains of our respective countrysides. The same ideals of an 'organic society' founded upon a guild-like co-operation have been put forward by thinkers in most advanced industrialised societies—West and East. At the same time, however, the images that are put forward by those producing popular cultural forms within Japan are remarkably similar to those that have over the decades been created by Westerners looking at Japan from the outside. It is clear that the Japanese are as prepared as ourselves to exoticise their surroundings, and we saw them indulging in a number of similar practices—whether in the context of developing tourist images or creating a media mosaic. In view of the fact that Japan is following the same path of (post-)industrial capitalism taken by Western European countries and the United States, it is perhaps not surprising to find such parallels. Let's face it, we are all trying to communicate through a 'language of modernity'.

This language, however, is not created in isolation (however much the 'noodle westerns' might like to portray society as 'untainted' and 'purely' Japanese). Since the latter half of the nineteenth century, Japan has been very closely connected with the West, and it is this contact with Western cultures which has—I would argue—affected the way in which the Japanese now see themselves. After all, it is surely not a coincidence that it was during this initial period of contact, specifically between the late 1880s and the death of the Emperor Meiji in 1912, that the language of modern ideology was born; then that Japan first produced its modern myths (Gluck 1985: 36–7).

And how did Westerners portray the Japanese? Very crudely, one can reply that they saw Japanese culture in terms of its *difference* from Western cultures. This was as true of anthropology as it was of art, and we find both anthropologists and artist-critics in the West emphasising this set of perceived differences when talking about Japan. It is these differences that have been picked up by the Japanese and reflected back on to the West. I have already argued that a society will always dictate anthropology's approaches to it, and that Japan is no exception to this rule: it has moulded our discipline in its own image, obliging us to talk of Japanese society as 'group' oriented, 'harmonious', 'homogeneous', even a 'shame' culture. In this respect Japan is opposed to the 'individual', 'conflict', 'plural', and 'guilt' type of culture seen to characterise the West. Moreover, we have frequently treated the Japanese as *if* they were a primitive, exotic people, thus practising the same kind of 'salvage' ethnography as the Japanese themselves when worshipping their past.

Such attitudes may also be found in Westerners' appreciation of the Japanese arts. Evett (1982: xiii) summarises well the ways in which artists and critics in the late nineteenth and early twentieth centuries idolised art and nature in Japan:

The Japanese approach to nature as the main topic of discussion and the avenues taken to explain it were both based on general Western perceptions of Japanese civilisation and the spirit of the Japanese people. Long-standing myth, often reinforced by biased travelers' reports, but nurtured mostly by an escapist longing for the opposite of advanced, complex Western civilisation, perpetuated a vision of the Japanese as simple, innocent, primitive people living in blissful harmony with gentle, nurturing, benign nature. The Japanese pictorial images of nature seemed in turn to confirm this picture, and an intricate set of intertwined observations and explanations of Japanese art and the people who created it produced a general view that the Japanese civilisation had been arrested in permanent infancy. Unlike the West, it had not experienced progressive development and had remained in its original state. This meant that the Japanese were like early man, living simply and in primitive, childlike rapport with nature.

The interesting point here is that a number of Westerners praised Japanese art for precisely the same reasons that William Morris in late-nineteenth-century Britain and Yanagi Sōetsu in early-twentieth-century Japan praised Gothic art: the Japanese were imbued with '*l'ame gothique*', in which everyone was organised along medieval principles (Jarves 1984: 24). They thus applied in *space* the same set of principles that were applied in *time* by propounders of the Arts and Crafts and Folk Craft movements.

At the same time, both anthropologists and Western artists saw the answer to their questions in the way in which the Japanese lived close to nature. Anthropologists explained many features of the 'group' model by examining man's relation to his environment in Japan; artists found a 'truly spiritual' art in man's subservience to nature. Both of these approaches led to theories emphasising the abnegation of the 'self'. Ultimately, they highlighted an opposition between Eastern intuition and Western rationalism which is typical not only of much writing about Japan but of orientalism in general.

Clearly, it was not only through anthropology and art that our Western images of Japan have been created. However the data presented here are sufficient, I think, to suggest that the ideals put forward by contemporary Japanese about their society and culture are firmly founded in *Western*, rather than in purely Japanese, images of Japan. Closeness to nature in *mingei* aesthetics is one obvious example. The use of the Tokugawa period in *jidaigeki* as an 'original state' is another. By being 'childlike', too, the Japanese can cleverly support an opposition between Western 'mind' and Japanese 'intuition', mentioned in my discussion of high school baseball, advertising slogans and pottery aesthetics. The concept of a 'gothic spirit' leads directly to an emphasis on 'feudal' types of social relation, epitomised by *giri* and *ninjō*.

All this leads me to argue with Said (1978: 5) that the relationship between the West and Japan is, like that between the Occident and the Orient as a whole, 'a relationship of power, of domination, of varying degrees of complex hegemony'. What makes Japan different from other parts of the Orient is that it appears to have developed in *nihonjinron*, or 'discussions of the Japanese', a means whereby it can practise on the West precisely that kind of orientalism from which it has had to suffer, and to some extent still suffers, at the hands of Westerners. By adopting orientalist tactics—such as, for example, a refusal to account for human plurality (*ibid.* 154)—and by giving *positive* values to characteristics like 'emotion' hitherto used as a form of denigration by Westerners writing on the Orient, the Japanese have turned the tables on their would-be material and spiritual conquerors.

It is for this reason that I strongly believe that those anthropologists and social acientists who try to discuss Japanese society and culture in terms of *nihonjinron* are not simply barking up the wrong bamboo. Rather, they have been catapulted into the inverse orientalist trap laid for them by the Japanese themselves. For our own intellectual health, we would be advised in future to avoid this trap. As I see it, the only way to do so is by trying to explain Japan according to theories that are if not universally, then at least generally, applicable. Whether this aim has been achieved in this book I am not sure, but I hope that at least the ground has been sufficiently prepared for others to do battle thereon. In the meantime, we should perhaps beware the joys of *pachinko* and pay more attention to the 'rustle of language' (Barthes 1986: 77–8) played by those slot machine balls. Who knows? One of the barbarians might one day hit the jackpot!

Bibliography

Abrahams, Roger 1974. 'Black talking on the streets'. In R. Bauman and R. Sherzer (eds.), *Explorations in the Ethnography of Speaking*. Cambridge: Cambridge University Press, pp. 240–62.

Anderson, J., and Richie, D. 1959. *The Japanese Film: art and industry*. Tokyo: Tuttle.

Ardener, Edwin 1971. 'Introductory essay'. In *idem*. (ed.), *Social Anthropology and Language*. A.S.A. Monographs 10. London: Tavistock, pp. ix-cii.

Austin, Lewis (ed.) 1976. *Japan: the paradox of progress*. New Haven and London: Yale University Press.

Bachnik, Jane 1982. 'Deixis and self/other reference in Japanese discourse.' *Sociolinguistic Working Paper 99*. Austin, Texas: Southwest Educational Development Laboratory.

Baerwald, Hans 1979. 'Parties, factions, and the Diet.' In Hyoe Murakami and Johannes Hirschmeier (eds.), *Politics and Economics in Contemporary Japan*. Second edition. Tokyo: Kodansha International, pp. 21–63.

Barthes, Roland 1972. *Mythologies*. London: Jonathan Cape.

Barthes, Roland 1986. *The Rustle of Language*. Oxford: Basil Blackwell.

Bataille, Georges 1965. *L'Erotisme*. Paris: Minuit.

Befu, Harumi 1974. 'An ethnography of dinner entertainment in Japan', *Arctic Anthropology*, volume XI (Supplement), pp. 196–203.

Befu, Harumi 1980. 'The group model of Japanese society and an alternative', *Rice University Studies*, volume 66, number 1, pp. 169–87.

Benedict, Ruth 1946. *The Chrysanthemum and the Sword*. Boston: Houghton Mifflin.

Berger, John 1972. *Ways of Seeing*. Harmondsworth: Pelican.

Bernstein, Basil 1971. *Class, Codes and Control*. New York: Schocken Books.

Bloch, Maurice 1975. 'Introduction', in *idem*. (ed.), *Political Language and Oratory in Traditional Society*. London: Academic Press, pp. 1–28.

Bloch, Maurice 1977. 'The past and the present in the present', *Man* n.s., volume 12, number 2, pp. 278–92.

Borgstrom, B.-E. 1984. 'Power structure and political speech', *Man* n.s., volume 19, number 2, pp. 313–27.

Bourdieu, Pierre 1984. *Distinction: a social critique of the judgement of taste*. Translated by Richard Nice. London: Routledge & Kegan Paul.

Bright, William (ed.) 1966. *Directions in Sociolinguistics*. The Hague: Mouton.

Brown, R. and Gilman, A. 1960. 'Pronouns of solidarity and power'. In T. Sebeok (ed.), *Style in Language*. Cambridge, Mass.: MIT Press, pp. 253–76.

Buruma, Ian 1984. *Behind the Mask: on sexual demons, sacred mothers, transvestites, gangsters and other Japanese heroes*. New York: Pantheon.

Chang, Carsun 1957. *The Development of Confucian Thought*. New York: Bookman Associates.

Clifford, James 1986. 'On ethnographic allegory'. In J. Clifford and G. Marcus (eds.), *Writing Culture: the poetics and politics of ethnography*. Berkeley and Los Angeles: University of California Press, pp. 98–121.

Cole, Robert 1971. *Japanese Blue Collar: the changing tradition*. Berkeley and Los Angeles: University of California Press.

Dalby, Liza 1983. *Geisha*. Berkeley and Los Angeles: University of California Press.

Dale, Peter 1986. *The Myth of Japanese Uniqueness*. London: Croom Helm.

Davis, John 1972. 'Gifts and the U.K. economy', *Man* n.s., volume 7, number 3, pp. 408–23.

de Bary, Wm Theodore 1979. 'Introduction' and 'Sagehood as a secular and spiritual ideal in Tokugawa Neo-Confucianism'. In de Bary and Bloom (eds.), *Principle and Practicality: essays in Neo-Confucianism and practical learning*. New York: Columbia University Press.

Doi, Takeo 1981. *The Anatomy of Dependence*. Tokyo: Kodansha International. Second edition.

Dore, Ronald 1958. *City Life in Japan*. Berkeley and Los Angeles: University of California Press.

Dore, Ronald 1965. 'The legacy of Tokugawa education'. In M. Jansen (ed.), *Changing Japanese Attitudes Toward Modernization*. Princeton, N.J.: Princeton University Press, pp. 99–131.

Eco, Umberto 1986. *Travels in Hyperreality*. Translated by William Weaver. New York: Harcourt Brace Jovanovich.

Economist, The 1988. 'Broadening the mind'. *The Economist*, volume 307, number 7549. 7 May 1988.

Evett, Elisa 1982. *The Critical Reception of Japanese Art in Late Nineteenth Century Europe*. Studies in the Fine Arts. The Avant-garde; Number 36. Ann Arbor: UMI Research Press.

Fischer, John 1964. 'Words for self and others in Japanese families', *American Anthropologist*, volume 66, number 6, pp. 115–26.

Frake, C. 1964. 'How to ask for a drink in Subanun', *American Anthropologist*, volume 66, number 6 (pt. 2, Special Publication), pp. 127–32.

Frager, Robert and Rohlen, Thomas 1976. 'The future of a tradition: Japanese spirit in the 1980s'. In L. Austin (ed.), *Japan: the paradox of progress*. New Haven and London: Yale University Press, pp. 255–78.

Fukutake, Tadashi 1967. *Asian Rural Society: China, India, Japan*. Tokyo: University of Tokyo Press.

Fung, Yu-lan 1953. *A History of Chinese Philosophy*, volume 2. Translated by Derek Bodde. London: Allen and Unwin.

Gather International 1972–73. *A Study of Japanese Travel Habits and Patterns*. Washington, DC: United States Travel Service.

Geertz, Clifford 1972. 'Linguistic etiquette'. In J. B. Pride and Janet Holmes (eds.), *Sociolinguistics*. Harmondsworth: Penguin Books. pp. 167–79 (excerpt from C. Geertz, *The Religion of Java*. New York: Free Press, 1960).

Geertz, Clifford 1983. *Local Knowledge: further essays in interpretive anthropology*. New York: Basic Books.

Girard, René 1977. *Violence and the Sacred*. Baltimore: Johns Hopkins Press.

Gluck, Carol 1985. *Japan's Modern Myths: ideology in the late Meiji period*. Princeton, N.J.: Princeton University Press.

Graburn, Nelson 1976 (ed.). *Ethnic and Tourist Arts: cultural expressions from the fourth world*. Berkeley and Los Angeles: University of California Press.

Graburn, Nelson 1977. 'Tourism: the sacred journey'. In V. Smith (ed.), *Hosts and Guests: the anthropology of tourism*. Philadelphia: University of Pennsylvania Press.

Graburn, Nelson 1983. *To Pray, Pay and Play: the cultural structure of Japanese tourism*. Aix-en-Provence: Centre des Hautes Etudes Touristiques.

Hamada, Shōji 1965. 'Onta no karausu hoka (Onta's clay crushers and other matters)', *Mingei* 147, pp. 8–9.

Hannerz, Ulf 1969. *Soulside*. New York: Columbia University Press.

Harries, Phillip 1989. 'A sense of tragedy: attitudes in Europe and Japan'. In A. Boscara (ed.), *Rethinking Japan*. Tenterden: Paul Norbury Publications, 1989.

Haug, Wolfgang 1986. *Critique of Commodity Aesthetics*. Translated by Robert Bock. Cambridge: Polity Press.

Hymes, Dell 1971. 'Sociolinguistics and the ethnography of speaking'. In E. Ardener (ed.), 1971. pp. 47–94.

Ide, Sachiko 1982. 'Japanese sociolinguistics, politeness and women's language', *Lingua*, volume 57, pp. 357–85.

Ide, Sachiko 1986. 'Introduction: the background of Japanese sociolinguistics', *Journal of Pragmatics*, volume 10, pp. 281–6.

Ishida, Takeshi 1984. 'Conflict and its accommodation: *omote-ura* and *uchi-soto* relations'. In E. Krauss, T. Rohlen and P. Steinhoff (eds.), *Conflict in Japan*. Honolulu: University of Hawaii Press, pp. 16–38.

Jakobson, Roman 1960. 'Closing statement: linguistics and poetics'. In T. Sebeok (ed.), *Style in Language*. Cambridge, Mass.: MIT Press.

Jarves, James 1984. *A Glimpse at the Art of Japan*. Rutland, Vermont and Tokyo: Charles E. Tuttle. (first published 1976)

Johnson, Chalmers 1980. '*Omote* (explicit) and *ura* (implicit): translating Japanese political terms', *Journal of Japanese Studies*, volume 6, number 1, pp. 89–115.

Keene, Donald 1972. 'Japanese aesthetics'. In *Landscapes and Portraits: appreciations of Japanese culture*. London: Secker and Warburg.

Kumon, Shumpei 1982. 'Some principles governing the thought and behavior of Japanists (contextualists)', *Journal of Japanese Studies*, volume 8, number 1, pp. 5–28.

Labov, William 1972. 'Rules for ritual insults'. In his *Language in the Inner City*. Oxford: Basil Blackwell, pp. 297–353.

Lakoff, George and Johnson, Mark 1980. *Metaphors We Live By*. Chicago: University of Chicago Press.

Lambert, W. G. 1972. *Language, Psychology and Culture*. Stanford: Stanford University Press.

Lebra, Takie Sugiyama 1976. *Japanese Patterns of Behavior*. Honolulu: East-West Center Press.

Leech, Geoffrey 1966. *English in Advertising*. London: Longman.

Lévi-Strauss, Claude 1966. *The Savage Mind*. London: Weidenfeld and Nicolson.

Loveday, Leo 1982. 'Japanese donatory forms: their implications for linguistic theory', *Studia Linguistica*, volume 36, number 1, pp. 39–63.

Loveday, Leo 1986. 'Japanese sociolinguistics: an introductory survey', *Journal of Pragmatics*, volume 10, pp. 287–326.

MacCannell, Dean 1976. *The Tourist: a new theory of the leisure class*. New York: Schocken Books.

Macfarlane, Alan 1985. 'The root of all evil'. In D. Parkin (ed.), *The Anthropology of Evil*. Oxford: Basil Blackwell, pp. 57–76.

McLuhan, Marshall 1964. *Understanding Media: the extensions of man*. New York: McGraw-Hill.

Marchand, Roland 1985. *Advertising the American Dream*. Berkeley and Los Angeles: University of California Press.

Martin, Samuel 1964. 'Speech levels in Japan and Korea'. In D. Hymes (ed.), *Language in Culture and Society*. New York: Harper and Row, pp. 407–15.

Martinez, D.P. 1989. 'Tourism and the *ama*: the search for the real Japan'. In E. Ben-Ari, B. Moeran and J. Valentine (eds.), *Unwrapping Japan*. Manchester: Manchester University Press.

Marvin, Garry 1986. 'Honour, integrity and the problem of violence in the Spanish bullfight'. In D. Riches (ed.), *The Anthropology of Violence*. Oxford: Basil Blackwell, pp. 118–35.

Mellon, J. 1976. *The Waves at Genji's Door*. New York: Pantheon.

Miller, Roy 1967. *The Japanese Language*. Chicago: University of Chicago Press.

Miller, Roy 1971. 'Levels of speech *(keigo)* and the Japanese linguistic response to modernization'. In D. Shively (ed.), *Tradition and Modernization in Japanese Culture*. Princeton: Princeton University Press, pp. 601–65.

Miller, Roy 1982. *Japan's Modern Myth: the language and beyond*. Tokyo and New York: Weatherhill.

Milner, George 1971. 'The quartered shield: outline of a semantic taxonomy'. In E. Ardener (ed.), *Social Anthropology and Language*. A.S.A. Monographs 10, London: Tavistock, pp. 243–69.

Mishima, Yukio 1977. *The Way of the Samurai*. New York: Pedigree.

Mizuo, Hiroshi 1966. 'Gendai to mingei (Folk crafts and the present)', *Geijutsu Shincho*, volume 17, number 5.

Mizuo, Hiroshi 1968. *Gendai mingeiron* (Current folk craft theory). Tokyo: Shin-chōsha.

Mizuo, Hiroshi 1971. 'Yakimono no bi—17: Onta (The beauty of pottery—17: Onta), *Nihon Bijutsu Kōgei* 392.

Moeran, Brian 1984. *Lost Innocence: folk craft potters of Onta, Japan*. Berkeley and Los Angeles: University of California Press.

Moeran, Brian 1985a. 'Inside out: spatial metaphors the Japanese live by'. Paper delivered at the Japan Anthropologists' Workshop, Oxford.

Moeran, Brian 1985b. *Ōkubo Diary: portrait of a Japanese valley.* Stanford: Stanford University Press.

Moeran, Brian 1987. 'The art world of contemporary Japanese ceramics', *Journal of Japanese Studies,* volume 13, number 1, pp. 27–50.

Morley, John David 1985. *Pictures from the Water Trade.* New York: Atlantic Monthly Press.

Morris, Ivan 1970. *The Pillow Book of Sei Shōnagon.* Harmondsworth: Penguin.

Mukarovsky, Jan 1976. 'Poetic reference'. In L. Matejka and I. Titunik (eds.), *Semiotics of Art.* Cambridge, Mass.: MIT Press, pp. 155–63.

Mukerjee, R. 1948. *The Social Function of Art.* Bombay: Hind Kitabs.

Nagara, Susumu 1972. *Japanese Pidgin English in Hawaii.* Honolulu: University of Hawaii Press.

Nagashima, Nobuhiro 1973. 'A reversed world: or is it? The Japanese way of communication and their attitudes towards alien cultures'. In R. Horton and R. Finnegan (eds.), *Modes of Thought.* London: Faber and Faber, pp. 92–111.

Nakane, Chie 1967. *Kinship and Economic Organization in Rural Japan.* London: Athlone Press.

Nakane, Chie 1970. *Japanese Society.* Berkeley and Los Angeles: University of California Press.

Needham, Rodney (ed.) 1973. *Right and Left: essays on dual symbolic classification.* Chicago: University of Chicago Press.

Neustupny, Jiri 1987. *Communicating with the Japanese.* Tokyo: The Japan Times.

Nihon Kōtsū Kōsha 1982. *Nyūsu to Shiryō* (News and Data), volume 2. Tokyo: Japan Travel Bureau.

Nishio, M. 1982. *Gifuto Māketingu* (Gift Marketing). Tokyo: Bijinesu-sha.

Niyekawa, Agnes 1984. 'Analysis of conflict in a television home drama'. In E. Krauss, T. Rohlen and P. Steinhoff (eds.), *Conflict in Japan.* Honolulu: University of Hawaii Press, pp. 61–84.

Parkin, David 1976. 'Exchanging words'. In B. Kapferer (ed.), *Transaction and Meaning,* (A.S.A. Essays 1). Philadelphia: ISHI.

Parkin, David 1978. *The Cultural Definition of Political Response.* London: Academic Press.

Parkin, David 1980. 'The creativity of abuse', *Man* n.s., volume 15, number 1, pp. 45–64.

Pateman, Trevor 1983. 'How is understanding an advertisement possible?' In H. Davis and P. Walton (eds.), *Language, Image, Media.* Oxford: Basil Blackwell.

Paulson, Joyce 1976. 'Evolution of the feminine ideal'. In J. Lebra, J. Paulson, and E. Powers (eds.), *Women in Changing Japan.* Colorado: Westview Press, pp. 1–24.

Posener, Jill 1982. *Spray it Loud.* London: Routledge and Kegan Paul.

Pratt, Mary 1986. 'Fieldwork in common places'. In J. Clifford and G. Marcus (eds.), *Writing Culture: the poetics and politics of ethnography.* Berkeley and Los Angeles: University of California Press, pp. 27–50.

Rappaport, Roy 1971. 'Nature, culture and ecological anthropology'. In H. L. Schapiro (ed.), *Man, Culture and Society.* Oxford: Oxford University Press.

Redfern, W. 1982. 'Guano of the mind: puns in advertising', *Language and*

Communication, volume 2, number 3, pp. 269–76.

Richie, Donald 1982. *The Japanese Movie*. Tokyo: Kodansha International.

Rosaldo, Michelle 1973. 'I have nothing to hide: the language of Ilongot oratory', *Language in Society*, volume 2, number 2, pp. 192–223.

Said, Edward 1978. *Orientalism*. New York: Pantheon Books.

Salmond, Anne 1975. 'Mana makes the man: a look at Maori oratory and politics'. In M. Bloch (ed.), *Political Language and Oratory in Traditional Society*. London: Academic Press, pp. 45–63.

Schodt, Frederik 1983. *Manga! Manga! The world of Japanese comics*. Tokyo: Kodansha International.

Scott-Stokes, H. 1974. *The Life and Death of Yukio Mishima*. New York: Farrar Straus and Giroux.

Sibata, Takeshi 1975. 'On some problems in Japanese sociolinguistics: reflections and prospect'. In F. Peng (ed.), *Language in Japanese Society*. Tokyo: University of Tokyo Press, pp. 159–73.

Smith, Robert 1978. *Kurusu: the price of progress in a Japanese village 1951–75*. London: Dawson.

Smith, Robert 1983. *Japanese Society*. Cambridge: Cambridge University Press.

Tanaka, Keiko 1989. '"Intelligent elegance": women in Japanese advertising'. In E. Ben-Ari, B. Moeran and J. Valentine (eds.), *Unwrapping Japan*. Manchester: Manchester University Press.

Tanaka, Takashi 1969. 'Onta e no osasoi (Invitation to Onta)', *Mingei* 195, pp. 44–8.

Tanaka, Toyotarō 1961. 'Kyūshu no minyō (Folk potteries in Kyushu)', *Mingei* 101, pp. 6–10.

Tanaka, Yōko 1965. 'Onta no tōgyō (Ceramic production in Onta)'. *Mingei* 147, pp. 17–25.

Tomars, Adolf 1940. *Introduction to the Sociology of Art*. Mexico City.

Tsunoda, R., de Barry, T., and Keene, D. (eds.) 1964. *Sources of Japanese Tradition*, volume 1. New York: Columbia University Press.

Tsurumi, Shunsuke 1987. *A Cultural History of Postwar Japan 1945–1980*. London: KPI.

Tucker, R. 1973. *Japan: film image*. London: Studio Vista.

Van Gulik, W. R. 1982. *Irezumi: the pattern of dermatography in Japan*. Leiden: E. J. Brill.

Vogel, Ezra 1963. *Japan's New Middle Class*. Berkeley and Los Angeles: University of California Press.

Wagatsuma, Hiroshi and DeVos, George 1967. 'The outcast tradition in modern Japan: a problem in social self-identity'. In R. Dore (ed.), *Aspects of Social Change in Modern Japan*. Princeton: Princeton University Press, pp. 373–407.

Weber, Max 1947. 'The social psychology of world religions'. In *From Max Weber—Essays in Sociology* (edited by C. Wright Mills and translated by H. Garth). London: Kegan Paul, Trench and Trubner.

Whiting, Robert 1977. *The Chrysanthemum and the Bat: baseball samurai style*. New York: Dodds, Mead & Co.

Williams, Raymond 1963. *Culture and Society 1780–1950*. Harmondsworth: Pelican.

Bibliography

Williams, Raymond 1976. *Communications*. Harmondsworth: Penguin.
Williams, Raymond 1980. 'Advertising: the magic system'. In his *Problems in Materialism and Culture*. London: Verso, pp. 170–95.
Williamson, Judith 1978. *Decoding Advertisements*. London: Marion Boyars.
Williamson, Judith 1987. *Consuming Passions: the dynamics of popular culture*. London: Marion Boyars.
Whorf, Benjamin 1956. *Language, Thought and Reality*. Cambridge, Mass.: MIT Press.
Yanagi, Sōetsu 1931. 'Hita no Sarayama', *Kōgei* 9, pp. 1–11.
Yanagi, Sōetsu 1932. 'Sakubutsu no kōhansei (The afterlife of crafts)', *Kōgei* 15, pp. 52–71.
Yanagi, Sōetsu 1954. *Nihon Mingeikan* (The Japan Folk Craft Museum). Tokyo: Nihon Mingeikan.
Yanagi, Sōetsu 1955. *Kōgei no michi* (The Way of Crafts). *Selected works*, volume 1. Tokyo: Nihon Mingeikan.
Yasuda, Teruo 1984. *Parodi Kōkoku Daizenshū* (Collection of Parody Advertisements). Tokyo: Seibundo Shinkosha.
Yazaki, Takaya and Yasuda, Teruo 1985. *Parodi CM Daizenshū* (Collection of Parody Commercials). Tokyo: Seibundo Shinkosha.
Yazaki, T. 1968. *Social Change and the City in Japan*. Tokyo: Japan Publications Inc.
Yoneyama, T. 1967. 'Kurikoma: a farm village in the mountains of the Tohoku district of north central Japan'. In J. Seward (ed.), *Contemporary Change in Traditional Societies*, volume 2. Urbana: University of Illinois Press.

Acknowledgements

Most of the material presented in this volume has already been published in journals or books, albeit in somewhat different form. A substantive part of Chapter 1 originally came out in the *Journal of Pragmatics*, volume 12, 1988. Chapter 2 was a seminar paper delivered at the Nissan Institute, Oxford, and to the Center for Japanese Studies at the University of California, Berkeley. It was later published in the *Journal of the Anthropological Society of Oxford*, volume 15 (1984), before being reprinted in Joy Hendry and Jonathan Webber (eds.), *Interpreting Japanese Society*, JASO, Oxford, 1986. Chapter 3 was published in *The Anthropology of Tourism*, edited by Nelson Graburn, *Annals of Tourism Research*, volume 10, 1983. Chapter 4 started out as a seminar paper given to the Department of Anthropology at the University of Manchester, before being published in *Man*, volume 19, number 2, 1984, Royal Anthropological Institute of Great Britain and Ireland Chapter 5 was first delivered at the Universities of California, Berkeley, and British Columbia in 1980, and then appeared in *Pacific Affairs*, Volume 54, in the following year. The chapter also makes use of material from my own book, *Lost Innocence: folk craft potters of Onta, Japan*, University of California Press, 1984. A lengthier version of Chapter 6 came out in *Asian Folklore Studies*, volume 57, 1987. Chapter 7 was published by *Language & Communication* volume 5, 1985, while the English data in Chapters 8 and 9 appeared in volume 4 of the same journal (1984), Pergamon Press PLC. Chapter 10 was first delivered at the seminar on Evil at the School of Oriental & African Studies in the spring of 1983, before being published in David Parkin (ed.), *Anthropology of Evil*, Basil Blackwell, 1985. Chapter 11 was given at the conference on Violence at St Andrew's University in January 1985 and was published in the following year in the volume edited by David Riches, *Anthropology of Violence*, Basil Blackwell. I am very grateful to all the publishers named above for permission to reprint my pieces in this book. Many people have contributed to it by their questions and comments after seminars, especially members of the Department of Anthropology Seminar at the Second of Oriental & African Studies, London. To them, and to David Parkin in particular, I would like to express my heartfelt gratitude.

B.D.A.M.

Index

Index

Index